COOKING
IN THE
SOUTH

with
Johnnie Gabriel

Photographs by ERIK BOKER

THOMAS NELSON
Since 1798

NASHVILLE   DALLAS   MEXICO CITY   RIO DE JANEIRO   BEIJING

Published in Nashville, Tennessee, by Thomas Nelson. Thomas Nelson is a registered trademark of Thomas Nelson, Inc.

Thomas Nelson, Inc. titles may be purchased in bulk for educational, business, fund-raising, or sales promotional use. For information, please e-mail SpecialMarkets@ThomasNelson.com.

Edited by Carol Boker

Library of Congress Cataloging-in-Publication Data

Gabriel, Johnnie, 1945–
  Cooking in the South with Johnnie Gabriel / edited by Carol Boker ; photographs by Erik Boker.
    p. cm.
  ISBN 978-1-4016-0405-9
  1. Cookery, American—Southern style. 2. Gabriel's Desserts (Restaurant) I. Boker, Carol. II. Title.
  TX715.2.S68G33 2008
  641.5975—dc22   2008007092

Printed in the United States of America

08 09 10 11 12 13 RRD 6 5 4 3 2 1

TABLE OF CONTENTS

FOREWORD

I can't tell y'all how happy I am to be writing this. Nothing makes me prouder than when someone near and dear to me succeeds at what they love to do. My cousin Johnnie has succeeded in so many ways already that when I found out she was publishing her very own cookbook, I was just beaming with pride. Now, for all y'all out there who aren't familiar with my family tree, here's the history.

Johnnie is actually my *first cousin once removed*. Don't ask me to explain that. She is my mama's first cousin, but she's nearer to me in age. Since I grew up in Albany, Georgia, and Johnnie grew up in Macon, Georgia, we didn't get to see each other that often. Of course, we saw each other at family reunions, and holiday gatherings. And every so often, usually in the summer, she and her family would come to Riverbend and spend time with my family. We'd swim and roller skate and just do what kids do in the summertime. We had a ball together. Now, she may not want me to tell this, but my favorite story of Johnnie and me will always be the leg-shaving story.

When I was ten, maybe eleven years old, I went to spend the week with Johnnie and her family in Macon. One night, she decided she was gonna teach me how to shave my legs. Now, a bar of soap, shaving cream, *water*, these are key ingredients to learn to shave. Johnnie didn't teach me with any of these key ingredients. Piled in the middle of the bed one night after everyone had gone to sleep, Johnnie handed me a single, straight-edged razor. Pulling the razor straight up my leg, I shaved both my legs for the first time. All the while, Johnnie assures me that was how you shave your legs. The next day, I woke-up and saw my legs. It looked like I had measles! Oh, my legs were so ugly, and they hurt, and I never wanted to shave my legs again! However, y'all will be happy to know that I did learn how to shave my legs correctly. My husband, Michael, may argue that I don't shave my legs as often as I should, but do I really need to now that I'm married?

As with most big families, Johnnie and I lost contact with each other over the years. I kept up with what she was doing, and she kept up with me, but it wasn't until I was hard at work on my third cookbook, *Just Desserts*, that I re-established contact. Knowing what a wonderful baker Johnnie is, it was only fitting that I ask her to contribute a recipe to the cookbook. Well, she was so gracious, she sent me not one, but several recipes for the cookbook. I published all of them. But, my favorite dessert has got to be her red velvet cake! It's just heaven on earth! Now, I don't say this about many recipes, but Johnnie's red velvet cake is better than mine! Johnnie made red velvet cupcakes for my brother Bubba's wedding in 2007, as well as an adorable overall cake for my darling grandson Jack. So, how good a baker is Johnnie? Well, aside from owning the successful Gabriel's Bakery in Marietta, Georgia, my darling husband Michael has a wish to be locked overnight inside Johnnie's bakery, with all of her deliciously sweet treats! I can't say I blame him for that!

I'm so thrilled Johnnie has decided to share some of her wonderful recipes with y'all. A talent like Johnnie's should be shared, and with as many people as possible. I hope y'all enjoy her cookbook, and her desserts, for many years to come.

—Paula Deen

Gabriel's Beginnings

The old cliché "necessity is the mother of invention" certainly fits the birth of Gabriel's Desserts. My family and I can't really decide when my husband, Ed, and I began baking cakes at home to sell, but we think it was 1989 or 1990. My oldest daughter, Stephanie, was married and living in Germany with her career military husband at the time. Laura, my youngest daughter, was at the University of Georgia.

When a deep real estate recession began in 1989, I was determined to see to it that Laura would be able to finish college. Laura was working two jobs and going to school, but it became apparent that I had to increase my income.

I approached Mary Moon, Marietta's "cake lady," to buy her recipes so I could "bake a few cakes" to pay Laura's apartment rent. Mary had been baking cakes for many years, ever since her husband was diagnosed with a terminal illness. She was ready to retire and insisted that she *give* the recipes to me. (Just maybe, there was another saint who touched my life.)

Little did I know what a great baker Ed Gabriel was! He kept telling me that he always baked with his mom. Ed and I both worked fulltime, he with remodeling projects and I at a friend's family business. With his more flexible schedule, he could be home earlier, so he began the baking. He could turn out some great pound and layer cakes. My job was to bake more and finish the cakes when I got home. Friends were delighted that they still had a source for Mary's delicious cakes, so our home baking project began. Ed and I baked nearly every night of the week and all day on Saturday. Laura's rent was paid, and she eventually made the Dean's List (once or twice) and graduated—a blessed day for our family.

A couple of years into our home baking project, John Moore of Moore, Ingram, Johnson and Steele, a large law firm here in Marietta, asked us to bake pound cakes for their clients for Christmas. We baked from our home kitchen, close to 100 pound cakes that Christmas for John. We're still baking cakes as gifts for their clients, around 200 each year.

In January 1996, I announced to Ed that I was either quitting baking at night or quitting my day job and opening a bakeshop. I had no idea what I was in for. Ed and I had lost everything but our home in the recession, so we had to borrow money to open the doors.

In December 1996, we opened Gabriel's Desserts on Whitlock Avenue with three employees. The shop sat perpendicular to the main street and had it not been for our reputation of the previous six years, community support, encouragement from friends, loyal employees, a seven-year note to Charter Bank, and the grace of God, I probably would have walked away and gone back to the corporate world. In that tiny space, we survived ten years—including ten Thanksgiving and Christmas holidays and eight wedding seasons. I realized we needed customers coming in daily, not just when they needed a dessert. Lunch would be a good time for that, so we added a deli in the space next door in 2004. We made soups, sandwiches, and fresh vegetables daily with twenty chairs for seating customers.

Simultaneously, my cousin Paula Deen was in Savannah building her restaurant business and reputation. Compared to Paula, I had it really easy in the years leading up to opening our businesses. As our reputation and business grew, we knew there was potential for much more in a better location and more space.

In February 2007, we opened new doors to Gabriel's Desserts in a location close to our original one. It has forty-eight hundred square feet on a site facing the main road, is beautifully decorated and equipped, and currently employs forty-two people.

Gabriel's Desserts has truly been a work in progress. I am learning that a business must always be evolving; if not, it is going backwards. It seems to work like the rest of life, keeping the good parts, ridding ourselves of the parts that don't work, and always on the lookout for quality ideas. Since I never intended to be in the restaurant business nor did my family own its own business, I haven't always possessed a "vision." Seeing a working model and reliance on intuition has helped me make good decisions for change. The idea for the most recent change occurred one afternoon around 5:50 PM. I was sitting in my office, which is glass and just off the main lobby so that I can help customers and see who comes and goes. I looked out into the lobby, and there were many customers trying to beat the 6 PM closing time to pick up takeout dinners. Not one chair in the dining room was occupied, but we had customers in line who would eat dinner with us if we were open. It occurred to me that I indeed owned a restaurant, not just a deli and

bakery. I thought, "What would Paula do with all those empty chairs?" She would fill them up three or four times a night I decided. After I consoled myself about the realization of owning a restaurant, I began to figure how to indeed be open in the evening.

Paula has stated several times that the hardest thing she has ever done is be in the food business. Nevertheless, here we both are! She is certainly having a great time and is an inspiration to anyone who is willing to work hard. We are now open for dinner four nights a week and feel that we meet a need in the community—a community that has opened its heart and pocketbook to us, for which we are truly grateful. Our desire is to continue to grow and improve with each and every passing day.

Marinated Shrimp (page 9)

APPETIZERS

Scrumptious Starts

BARBEQUED SHRIMP

Bill Dunaway, a friend and presently mayor of Marietta, Georgia, prepared this recipe for us at his lake house. I just don't eat unpeeled, deveined shrimp, but these I couldn't stop devouring when he passed the dish around. Soaking or marinating the shrimp in this mixture for twenty-four hours softens the shells. Bill says the brave will eat them—shell, tail and all. They are better tasting that way and a good source of calcium.

5	pounds small gray or pink shrimp (31-35 count), unpeeled	3	tablespoons (or more) Old Bay seasoning
	Canola oil	1	handful dried bay leaves, crumbled
8	to 12 ounces Worcestershire sauce	1½	to 2 ounces lemon juice
1½	to 2 ounces Tabasco sauce		Hickory chips
½	box Zatarains crab boil		
3	tablespoons (or more) ground black pepper		

In a plastic container combine the shrimp and enough oil to barely cover the shrimp. Add the Worcestershire, Tabasco, crab boil, black pepper, Old Bay seasoning, bay leaves, and lemon juice. Mix well, cover, and refrigerate. After 1 hour, check the mixture for spiciness. (After smoking the shrimp, the spice will be milder than during the marinating process. In order to have spicy shrimp, some heat should be present while the shrimp are marinating. Additional Tabasco sauce or black pepper may be needed at this point.) Refrigerate for 24 hours, mixing well every 4 to 6 hours.

Drain the shrimp in a colander. Place the shrimp in an electric or charcoal smoker without water in the pan. Use soaked hickory chips in the smoker for flavoring. Smoke the shrimp for approximately 45 minutes until they are pink.

Makes 15 to 20 appetizers or 10 entrées

THE DUNAWAYS

ill Dunaway's family owned and operated the wonderful 1848 House Restaurant in Marietta for twelve years. Cooking and enjoying good food is an art to his family. Bill's oldest daughter, Dawn, is a trained pastry chef and married Tom McEachern, well-known executive chef of Rays on the River, Atlanta and recipient of a James Beard award. (Several of Tom's recipes are included in this book.) Second daughter, Ann Dunaway Teh, earned a masters degree in nutrition,

and third daughter, Claire, an artist and teacher, is keenly interested in healthy, nutritional eating. Bill's wife, Dot, is also a good cook and one of the most gracious hostesses. Dot is the cog in this wheel, supporting and encouraging the family members in all their pursuits. An invitation to their home or lake house promises a culinary experience—good food and wine and lively company.

SHRIMP COCKTAIL WITH REMOULADE SAUCE

Fred King, a friend and a semi-retired vascular surgeon in Marietta, contributed this recipe. He now just works a couple of days a week and has time to play golf, hunt, and cook a lot.

1½	cups real mayonnaise	2	tablespoons diced garlic
½	cup Creole mustard	¼	cup chopped fresh
1	tablespoon Worcestershire sauce		parsley or ⅛ cup dried
1	teaspoon Tabasco	½	tablespoon lemon juice
½	cup diced green onions	2	tablespoons paprika
¼	cup celery		Salt and pepper, to taste

Combine the mayonnaise, mustard, Worcestershire sauce, Tabasco, diced green onions, celery, garlic, parsley, lemon juice, paprika, and salt and pepper in a blender and process until smooth. Chill well. Serve with large, peeled, deveined, cooked shrimp.

Makes about 3 cups sauce

MARINATED SHRIMP

See the photo on page 4.

Marinade

1¼	cups virgin olive oil
¾	cup warmed white vinegar
1½	teaspoons salt
2½	teaspoons celery seed
2½	tablespoons capers and juice
	Dash of hot sauce
¼	cup Worcestershire sauce
1	tablespoon yellow mustard

Shrimp

3	quarts (12 cups) water
6	to 10 peppercorns
⅛	teaspoon black pepper
	Juice and rind of 1 lemon
15	to 20 whole cloves

15	to 20 whole allspice
6	garlic cloves, minced
3	small onions, sliced
2	celery stalks, chopped or broken into pieces
2	bay leaves
1	fresh sprig thyme or ¼ teaspoon dried thyme
3	to 5 fresh parsley sprigs
	Small pinch of dried red pepper
1	tablespoon Worcestershire sauce
2	to 2½ pounds raw shrimp
4	medium onions, thinly sliced
1	box of bay leaves
	Lemons, for garnish

Prepare the marinade: In a medium bowl whisk together the olive oil, vinegar, salt, celery seed, capers, hot sauce, Worcestershire sauce, and yellow mustard until smooth.

Prepare the shrimp: In a large stockpot combine the 3 quarts water, peppercorns, black pepper, juice and rind of a lemon, the cloves, allspice, garlic cloves, 3 small onions, celery, 2 bay leaves, thyme, parsley, red pepper, and Worcestershire sauce. Bring to a rolling boil. Add about ¾ pound of the shrimp and return to a rolling boil. When the shrimp float to the top and turn pink they are ready to remove. Remove with a slotted spoon and move to a colander in the sink to drain and cool. Repeat the process until all the shrimp are cooked. When they are cool enough, peel and devein the shrimp.

In a nonmetallic pan layer the shrimp, 4 medium onions, and box of bay leaves, pouring the marinade over each layer. Cover and refrigerate for 24 hours.

When ready to serve, arrange the shrimp in a large serving bowl, removing the bay leaves. Garnish with lemon slices. Serve with cocktail picks.

Makes 10 to 12 servings

MARINATED VIDALIA ONIONS

2 cups water
1 cup apple cider vinegar
½ cup sugar
4 Vidalia onions, peeled and sliced
thinly

2 cups mayonnaise
Celery salt, to taste
Saltine crackers

In a medium mixing bowl, whisk together the water, vinegar, and sugar until the sugar dissolves. Place the onion slices in a 13 x 9-inch baking dish. Pour the marinade over the onions, tossing to coat well. Refrigerate the onions overnight.

Drain the onions, reserving the marinade for other purposes. In a medium bowl mix the onions with the mayonnaise. Add celery salt, to taste. Serve the onions in a large bowl. Set the bowl on a platter surrounded by crackers. Spoon onions over a few crackers and place on a plate to demonstrate the serving procedure.

Makes 6 to 8 servings

Cheddar Cheese and Bacon Spread

My late friend Dana Cain Hagood—a wonderful cook who loved to entertain and share her beautiful home—gave me this recipe.

8 ounces Cheddar cheese, grated	2 ounces chopped almonds
8 strips cooked bacon, crumbled	Mayonnaise or light mayonnaise
2 to 3 green onions, thinly sliced, include some green tops	

In a medium bowl mix the cheese, bacon, onions, and almonds. Add enough mayonnaise so the mixture is a good consistency for dipping. Serve with vegetables, crackers, or chips. Refrigerate any leftover spread. May be prepared a day ahead.

Makes about 2 cups

TOASTED PECANS

This is really simple but really delicious! It was given to me years ago by a family friend, Janis Portier.

½   cup butter or margarine, melted
3   cups pecan halves
      Salt, to taste

Preheat the oven to 275 degrees. Place the butter in a microwave-safe container. Melt the butter in the microwave oven. Arrange the pecan halves in a single layer on a cookie sheet. Drizzle the melted butter over the pecans and toss them to coat evenly. Add salt to taste. Roast the pecans for 30 minutes, stirring occasionally. Cool and store in an airtight container for up to two weeks.

Makes 3 cups

Cheese Straws

A truly Southern delicacy, cheese straws adorn our chicken and tuna salad lunch plates at Gabriel's.

1	pound New York sharp Cheddar cheese	3$\frac{1}{2}$	cups all-purpose flour
1$\frac{1}{2}$	cups (3 sticks) butter or margarine, at room temperature	1	teaspoon salt
		$\frac{1}{2}$	teaspoon red pepper flakes
			Paprika for color

Preheat the oven to 400 degrees. Grate the cheese in a food processor or by hand. Place the cheese in a large mixing bowl and allow it to come to room temperature. Add the butter and, with the mixing paddle, beat with the cheese.

In a large bowl sift together the flour, salt, and red pepper. Add the flour mixture to the cheese and butter mixture, combining well. Place the mixture in a cookie press and pipe 3-inch to 4-inch strips onto an ungreased cookie sheet. Sprinkle with the paprika. Bake for 8 to 10 minutes.

Makes 12 dozen

CHEESE STRAWS

outhern to the bone are cheese straws, cheese wafers, cheese crackers, and cheese crisps. All have the same basic ingredients with slight variations. On one recipe website alone, there were 146 recipes for cheese straws.

A sharp Cheddar cheese and flour are the main ingredients, but some folks have even strayed from using Cheddar cheese. Some recipes are too spicy, not spicy enough, too dry, piped too wide, and someone has even concocted a way to add rice cereal and pecans.

Cheese straws are piped from a bag, rolled into a ball and smashed flat, or rolled into a log and sliced and baked. Some companies have been established just to bake and sell cheese straws. In other words, there are several methods of preparation, different looks and ways to procure our beloved cheese straws. I am of the traditional persuasion; mine are about 3 to 3 $\frac{1}{2}$ inches long and no more than $\frac{1}{2}$ inch wide. Of course, I'm prejudiced and think Gabriel's are the best!

Cheese straws are served on all sorts of occasions: baby and wedding showers, graduations, brunches, dinner and cocktail parties, receptions, birthdays, baptisms, and political functions. At Gabriel's we serve them with our chicken and tuna salad dishes, and we also sell them by the dozen. They are supposed to be eaten at room temperature, but my husband, Ed, will eat them right out of the freezer. I have to hide them if I bring them home to serve at an upcoming occasion.

I found a recipe dating back to a cookbook published in 1894* and don't know if that was truly the first recipe. If so, someone evidently brought it South, and we adopted cheese straws as one of our food standards. If someone "pipes" a cheese straw for you, consider it a labor of love and pride. I'm just happy that someone concocted the first one to give us this delicacy.

* Recipes Tried and True, *compiled by the Ladies' Aid Society of the First Presbyterian Church, Marion, Ohio, 1894.*

CRAB DIP SUPREME

This is my favorite crab appetizer.

1	(8-ounce) package cream cheese, softened	8	ounces fresh crabmeat
2	tablespoons milk	2	ounces sliced almonds, toasted
1	tablespoon horseradish		Paprika
2	tablespoons minced scallions or green onions		

Preheat the oven to 350 degrees. Coat a small baking dish with nonstick cooking spray. In a small bowl combine the cream cheese, milk, and horseradish, mixing well. Add the scallions. Fold in the crabmeat. Spread the crab mixture evenly on the bottom of the prepared baking dish. Top with the toasted almonds and sprinkle with paprika. Bake for 20 minutes. Serve with crackers of your choice.

Makes 8 servings

Photograph by Christine Hall

My Cousin, Paula Deen

Growing up, little did I know that I was spending time with a relative that would come to be loved by so many in America. She was cute, fun, and energetic then, just as she is now. Mischievous would be a good word also. I knew her as Paula Hiers, but she's the now-famous Southern cook Paula Deen.

I was only about seven years old, so my recollections of trips to Albany are a little sketchy. I am two years older than Paula, but she has always seemed to be more savvy about the world. She grew up with her parents and grandparents owning their own businesses. As a small business owner now, I can only imagine how hardworking and tenacious they had to be in the 1940s and 50s. Paula's maternal grandfather—who I called Uncle Johnny—and my maternal grandmother—Mommee—were brother and sister. I was told that I was named after Uncle Johnny and my paternal grandfather, John Price Howell.

The story as I heard it was that Uncle Johnny and Aunt Irene had given shelter to my grandmother, grandfather, and their two children when they lost their farm in the 1920s. Paula speaks of her grandmother's restaurant in Hapeville, and it must have been at that time they came to my grandparents' rescue. The businesses that I have fond memories of are the motel, restaurant, skating rink, and pool that Uncle Johnny and Aunt Irene owned at River Bend just south of Albany. Paula's parents had a gas station and convenience store across the street from the motel.

My grandparents, Mommee and Poppee, never recovered financially from losing their old home place in Leesburg, Georgia, just north of Albany. When they moved back to Albany, they rented a room from a cousin who lived in a large, old home right across the street from the Albany Zoo. Can you imagine what that meant to a young girl visiting her grandparents for a couple of weeks during the summer—with the zoo and relatives that had what seemed like a huge swimming pool, a skating rink, and a restaurant? Mom always worked, and it was a real challenge to provide care for me during the summer. My sister, Kay, is seven years older than me, and I was more than she could deal with all summer. A couple of weeks with both grandmothers was a godsend to us all.

I would spend the day with Paula and Trina, Paula's aunt who was only about five years older than Paula. When I look back, I thought they were the dynamic duo. I remember that I was envious of Paula's having Corrie, her mother, at home all the time. Corrie was so sweet and giving. The only reprimand I remember Paula ever getting was Corrie sweetly saying, "Now, Paula Ann, you know you all shouldn't do so and so."

Paula and Trina, being real veterans of their very own "amusement park," had a lot of skills I didn't have. One of them was swimming. Their method of teaching me to swim was to throw me in the pool. I "dog paddled" back to the side and don't remember if I ever officially learned to swim in that pool or not. I recall the fun days of roller skating and, in general, bugging the staff in the

Photograph by Christine Hall

restaurant to keep us in hot dogs and French fries. It seemed to me that Paula and Trina had a lot of freedom and responsibility at the same time.

When I wasn't at River Bend, I was in Albany with a devoted grandmother and grandfather. One of Mommee's hobbies was painting. I think she might have been quite good had she the luxury of instruction and time to pursue art. We spent time drawing and painting during the day, and in the afternoon when Poppee came home, we walked over to the zoo. I never wanted those memorable summer vacations to end.

As we grew older and more involved with our own activities, my visits to River Bend ended. Paula visited me in Macon where I lived when I was in my early teens. As I remember, we talked about "girl stuff" and listened to records. She has reminded me that I was the person who first instructed her on her *need* to shave her legs and *how* to do it without a mother's permission. We took a razor blade, probably a used one from my dad, and hid under the bed sheets and shaved our legs. Her legs were fire-engine red the next day from using a dry razor blade on them. I've seen later photos of her legs. She has great legs. We didn't do any permanent damage!

Apple and Cinnamon Muffins (page 26)

BREADS AND BREAKFASTS

Early Rising

Pumpkin Bread

Nonstick cooking spray
4 cups all-purpose flour
$2/3$ teaspoon baking powder
$2^{1}/4$ teaspoons baking soda
$1^{1}/2$ teaspoons salt
1 teaspoon cinnamon
1 teaspoon cloves
$1/2$ teaspoon ginger
$1/2$ teaspoon allspice
5 large eggs
$3^{1}/2$ cups sugar
3 cups pumpkin
$1^{1}/3$ cups oil
$3/4$ cup cold water

Preheat the oven to 325 degrees. Coat three 9 x 5-inch loaf pans with nonstick cooking spray. In a large bowl, sift together the flour, baking powder, baking soda, salt, cinnamon, cloves, ginger, and allspice.

In another large bowl, beat the eggs well. Add the sugar, mixing well. Add the pumpkin, the oil, and the water, beating well to thoroughly combine. Add the dry ingredients to the egg mixture and mix well. Spoon the batter into the prepared pans, filling about two-thirds full. Bake for
1 hour.

Makes 3 loaves

CORNBREAD MUFFINS

1 cup vegetable shortening
2½ cups self-rising cornmeal mix
(we use White Lily)
¼ cup plus 1½ tablespoons all-purpose
flour

¾ cup sugar
½ cup mayonnaise
3 large eggs
1 quart (4 cups) buttermilk

Preheat the oven to 425 degrees. Heavily grease the inside of a muffin tin with the vegetable shortening. (You should be able to see clumps of shortening on the tins not just an even coating). In a large bowl, combine the cornmeal mix, flour, and sugar. Add the mayonnaise, eggs, and buttermilk. Whisk to mix well. Using an ice cream scoop, ladle the batter into the muffin cups, filling about three-fourths full. Bake for 18 to 20 minutes, or until the muffins are golden in color.

Makes 10 muffins

NO-COOK STRAWBERRY JELLY

My friend Merdean Baker Bone has made this jelly for years. Her children won't eat any other variation except this one.

2 cups pureed fresh or frozen
strawberries
4 cups sugar

1 box Sure-Jell
⅔ cup water

In a large bowl mix the pureed berries with the sugar. In a small saucepan stir together the Sure-Jell and the water. Bring the mixture to a boil and boil for 1 minute, stirring constantly. Pour the Sure-Jell into the berry mixture and stir thoroughly for approximately 3 minutes. Pour into jelly jars and tighten the lids immediately. Let the jelly sit at room temperature for 6 to 8 hours and then refrigerate.

Makes about 6 half-pint jars

APPLE AND CINNAMON MUFFINS

See the photo on page 22.

3	cups all-purpose flour	4	large eggs, lightly beaten
¾	teaspoon salt	1	cup buttermilk
2	teaspoons baking soda	3	cups finely chopped, unpeeled apples
2	cups vegetable shortening	2	teaspoons ground cinnamon
4	cups sugar, divided		

Preheat the oven to 350 degrees. Coat 48 tin muffin cups with nonstick cooking spray. In a medium bowl stir together the flour, salt, and baking soda and set aside. In a large bowl beat the shortening with a mixer until light and fluffy. Gradually add 3 cups of the sugar, beating on medium speed until well combined. Scrape down the sides of the bowl. Beat 2 more minutes. Add the eggs, one at a time, beating after each addition. With the mixer on low speed, add the flour mixture alternately with the buttermilk, beginning and ending with the flour mixture. Fold in the apples. Fill the prepared muffin cups two-thirds full.

In a small bowl mix the remaining 1 cup of sugar and the cinnamon. Using a teaspoon lightly sprinkle a small amount of the cinnamon-sugar mixture over the top of the unbaked muffins. Set aside the remaining cinnamon-sugar mixture.

Bake for 18 to 20 minutes or until golden brown and a tester inserted in the centers comes out clean. (Muffins will not rise high in the middle as other muffins do.) Cool in a pan on a wire rack for 15 minutes. Carefully remove the muffins from the cups (they will be tender). While still warm, roll the muffins in the remaining cinnamon-sugar mixture.

Makes 48 muffins

MAPLE WALNUT SCONES

2	pounds bread flour	1	cup firmly packed brown sugar
3½	tablespoons baking powder	20	ounces sour cream
1	tablespoon salt	2	tablespoons maple syrup
1¼	cups walnuts or pecans, toasted	1	large egg white, lightly beaten
1½	cups (3 sticks) butter		

Preheat the oven to 375 degrees. In a medium bowl sift together the flour, baking powder, and salt. Add the toasted nuts to the flour mixture and set aside. In a large bowl beat the butter and brown sugar. Add the sour cream and maple syrup. Mix until just combined. Add the dry ingredients and stir until the mixture just comes together.

Turn the dough onto a lightly floured board and roll out to a 1½-inch thickness. Cut the dough into rounds or triangles. Place on a nonstick cookie sheet. Brush the tops with the egg white and bake for 8 to 10 minutes or until the scones begin to turn golden.

Makes 24 scones

ICE BOX ROLLS

My friend Estelle Bogle makes these rolls and gives them as Christmas gifts. Estelle is known around Marietta for her delicious homemade rolls, as was her mother, Frances Elliott, who handed down to her daughter not only the art of roll-making but also the gift of sharing them with friends. To receive a tin with a big red bow from Estelle means there will be delicious rolls on your Christmas table.

2	(1/4-ounce) packages active dry yeast	2	large eggs
1	cup warm water (105 to 115 degress)	1	teaspoon baking soda
1	cup vegetable shortening, chopped into pieces	1	teaspoon baking powder
		1	tablespoon salt
3/4	cup sugar	7	cups sifted all-purpose flour
1	cup boiling water		(we use White Lily)

In a small bowl combine the yeast with the warm water. Stir with a spoon. If the yeast is active, bubbles and foam will start to form. In a large bowl combine the shortening, the sugar, and the boiling water, stirring with a spatula to mix but not completely dissolve the shortening. (Some lumps of shortening are allowed in this mixture.) Let cool.

When cool, add the eggs and the yeast mixture. Sift the baking soda, baking powder, and salt with 2 to 3 cups of the flour and add it to the large bowl, mixing and stirring with a spatula to incorporate it. Add 2 to 3 more cups flour, repeating the process of combining the two. When close to adding the final cup, you'll need to make a judgment call as to whether to use the last full cup or a little less. Touch the dough with your fingertips. When little bits of the dough stick to your fingers, it has enough flour. (The dough should still be sticky when you put it in the fridge to rise.) When you have determined that you have enough flour, cover the bowl with an airtight lid or with plastic wrap and place in the refrigerator at least overnight. (Dough will keep for up to five days in this stage.)

Cover the countertop with all-purpose, unsifted flour where you are going to roll out the rolls. The dough is still sticky and will absorb some of this flour on the countertop as you roll it. Spread flour up and down your rolling pin. Dip your round cutter or biscuit cutter into the flour so that the dough will release from the cutter. Work with half of the dough at a time. Knead the dough, pressing it with your fingertips around the outside edges; form a ball, tucking in all the loose "tails" of dough. The more you handle yeast roll dough, the lighter the rolls. That is the opposite of biscuit dough . . . the more you handle it the tougher the biscuits.

After kneading, shape the dough into a smooth, rounded ball. With a rolling pin, roll the dough to $1/4$ inch thick. With a floured cutter, cut out the circles as close together as possible without overlapping the edges. When the dough is completely covered with cut circles, remove the pieces of dough that are not cut into the circles and set aside to roll out again into more rolls.

Spread a light coat of vegetable shortening on the bottom and slightly up the sides of your sheet pan. (Use a disposable pan with a cover if you want to freeze until ready to use or give as gifts). Lift the cutout rolls one at a time, lightly dipping one end of the roll into a bowl of liquid oil. In the same motion stretch them a little to the point that they are no longer round but more of an oval. Fold the top third of the roll down and toward the center of the roll to form a Parker house roll.

Place the rolls in the pan, beginning in one corner and continuing them side by side and row under row, leaving no space between them. Completely fill the pan. When the pan is full, place it in a warm spot and cover with a towel. Let rise for 4 to 5 hours, avoiding any spots where they might be in a draft. They will rise in a room with a temperature in the high 60s but with no drafts. The tails of dough left from cutting out the rolls can be kneaded back together and rolled out on the flour-covered board, repeating the cutting, panning, and baking process.

Follow the above procedure with the remaining half of the dough. Preheat the oven to 400 degrees. Bake until slightly browned on top and bottom if you want to freeze to use at a later date. Set the pan aside for the rolls to cool. Then cover the pan and freeze. When ready to use, preheat the oven and pop them in long enough to brown and reheat.

If eating immediately, cook the rolls until lightly browned. Serve hot with real butter.

Makes 5 dozen rolls

PEAR HONEY

Beth Reid Banks shared this recipe with me. It was handed down from her mother, Frances White Reid. Frances was my sister Kay's mother-in-law, whose family somewhat "adopted" my girls and me when my first husband died at age thirty-one. At that time in my family, there were three generations of women who were widowed: my mother, grandmother, and I. The Reids generously gave of themselves, and I have bittersweet memories of those times. Frances also shared with us her jars of pear honey that she made with fruit from her yard. She was of the generation that let nothing go to waste. There's more to be learned than recipes from that generation and era.

8 cups grated peeled pears	4–6- pint sized canning jars, lids, and rings,
4 cups sugar	or 8–12 half-pint jars, lids, and rings
1 (20-ounce) can crushed pineapple, undrained	(You can purchase these from most grocery stores.)

Put the grated pears, sugar, and pineapple in a 6-quart heavy-duty stockpot. Bring to a boil, simmering for several hours until the pears are tender. The pears will turn a golden color.

While pears are simmering prepare the jars, rings, and lids according to the manufacturer's directions, washing them in hot soapy water and rinsing well. Check the jars for chips and the lids and rings for any dents or rust as these will prevent them from sealing correctly. Do not use other glass food jars, such as mayonnaise and pickle jars, since the seals are more likely to fail and the jars may break. Pour the hot pears into hot canning jars, closing with the rings and the lids. To insure proper sealing continue to process the jars in a boiling water bath.*

For the water bath, use a heavy-duty stockpot, tall enough for the water level to be several inches over the tops of the jars and large enough to allow the water to boil freely. Place a metal rack with dividers in the bottom of the stockpot and place the filled jars in the water bath when the water is hot but not boiling. U se a tight fitting lid and a metal rack with dividers to separate the jars and keep them off the bottom of the stockpot. With the lid on, boil the filled jars for approximately 20 minutes. Turn off the heat and allow the water to cool enough to safely handle the jars. Using tongs, carefully remove the jars from the water and allow to cool. As the jars begin to cool you may hear a "ping" from the lids as they seal or see a slight indention in the lids. Dry off the jars, (you may remove the rings if you like), label and date the jars and store in a cool, dry dark place until ready to enjoy.

Canned foods properly sealed will keep for several years. If the jar has been sealed properly, the lid will have to be removed by using a bottle opener. If the jar was not sealed properly there will be signs of spoilage. Do not eat the food if there is an odor, a foam on top, or mold. Discard any other jars that might spurt when opened, have bulging lids or any that have leaked.

* If you buy a home canner or borrow one, follow the manufacturer's directions. You may use a steam pressure canner, but steam canning is not necessary with high-acid foods such as pears.

Makes 4 to 6 pints or 8 to 12 half-pints

NOTE: Grate the pears with the grater blade of a food processor.

ORANGE BUTTER

This simple recipe adds the most delicious flavor to biscuits and cornbread, or refresh an old pound cake slice in a toaster oven and spread the butter over it while warm.

1 cup (2 sticks) butter, softened	½ cup orange juice
½ cup confectioners' sugar	

In a medium mixing bowl combine the butter and confectioners' sugar using an electric mixer fitted with a whip. On a slower speed, beat in the orange juice until the mixture is light and fluffy. Orange butter will keep in the refrigerator for several weeks.

Makes about 2 cups

BACON AND BLUE CHEESE STRATA

1	large loaf sliced white bread, crusts removed	2	cups whipping cream
1	pound bacon, cooked and drained	2	cups milk
1	pound Brie cheese with rind removed, cut into small pieces	10	large eggs
½	pound blue cheese, crumbled	2	teaspoons salt
2	tablespoons dried rosemary or sage	1	teaspoon black pepper
		10	drops hot sauce

Grease the bottom and sides of a 14 x 11-inch casserole dish. Cut the bread to fit the bottom, lining it completely. Layer with one-third of the bacon, cheeses, and rosemary. Repeat the layers, starting with the bread, two more times. In a medium bowl, whisk together the cream, milk, eggs, salt, pepper, and hot sauce. Pour evenly over the casserole. Press down lightly with a spatula. The bread should be thoroughly wet. Cover with plastic wrap. Refrigerate overnight. If bread is not thoroughly wet when ready to bake, add more cream and egg mixture.

Preheat the oven to 350 degrees. Bake the strata on the center rack of the oven for approximately 1 hour, or until the eggs are set.

Makes 6 to 8 servings

BREAKFAST BISCUIT WITH BACON AND TOMATO

8   slices bacon, cooked and drained
1   medium tomato, seeded and chopped
½   cup chopped sweet onion
3   ounces Swiss cheese, grated
½   cup mayonnaise
1   teaspoon dried basil
⅓   cup slivered almonds, chopped
15   frozen buttermilk biscuits, thawed and sliced horizontally

Preheat the oven to 375 degrees. Spray two mini muffin pans with nonstick cooking spray. Coarsely chop the bacon in a food processor or by hand and set aside. In a medium bowl mix the bacon, tomato, onion, cheese, mayonnaise, basil, and almonds. Line the mini muffin cups with the sliced biscuits, pressing to bottom and sides of each cup. Fill the cups with the bacon mixture. Bake for 10 to 12 minutes or until golden brown.

Makes 30 breakfast biscuits

CHEESE CLOUD

My friend Marcelle David passed along this really light breakfast dish. This was always our family's Christmas morning breakfast as my daughters were growing up. When Stephanie, my oldest daughter, married a career Army officer, Vernon Bahm, and moved to Germany, we had to change our traditional dish. None of us had the heart to have it without her. When I get lucky and both daughters are home for Christmas, Cheese Cloud is a must. It makes a wonderful brunch by adding fresh fruit, slices of ham, mini blueberry muffins, and a lemon-glazed pound cake.

12	slices of day-old white bread	1	tablespoon grated onion
½	pound Cheddar cheese, sliced (use bulk cheese, not processed)	¼	teaspoon salt
			Dash of cayenne pepper
4	large eggs		Dash of black pepper
2½	cups milk	1	teaspoon seasoned salt
½	teaspoon prepared yellow mustard		

Grease an 8 x 12-inch baking dish. Trim the crust from the bread and arrange 6 slices on the bottom of the prepared baking dish. Cover the bread with the cheese slices. Add the remaining bread slices. In a medium bowl whisk the eggs, milk, mustard, onion, salt, cayenne pepper, black pepper, and seasoned salt. Pour over the bread and cheese and let stand for 1 hour. (This dish may be prepared the day before and refrigerated overnight.)

Preheat the oven to 325 degrees. Bake the casserole 1 hour. Serve immediately.

Makes 6 servings

CHEESE GRITS WITH PANCETTA

3	ounces pancetta, bacon, or prosciutto, minced	1½	teaspoons Worcestershire sauce
4	cups water	1	teaspoon hot pepper sauce
1	cup quick-cooking grits	1¼	cups shredded white sharp Cheddar cheese, divided
1	teaspoon salt	1	tablespoon sherry
6	tablespoons butter	1	large egg, beaten

Preheat the oven to 300 degrees. Grease a 2½-quart baking dish. In a small skillet over medium heat, sauté the pancetta until crisp. Remove the pancetta from the pan with a slotted spoon and place on paper towels to drain. In a large saucepan bring the 4 cups water to a boil. Whisk in the grits and the salt, mixing well. Cook over low heat for 5 minutes or until most of the water is absorbed. Stir in the butter, Worcestershire, hot sauce, 1 cup of the cheese, and the sherry. Fold in the egg and pancetta until well combined. Spoon the mixture into the prepared baking dish. Sprinkle with the remaining cheese. Bake for 1 hour or until bubbly.

Makes 6 to 8 servings

NOTE: This dish may be prepared 1 day in advance and refrigerated. Bring to room temperature and bake just before serving.

Raspberry Grits

Grits is a long-standing Southern breakfast staple but has become a chic side dish as well, served with meats and seafood. Shrimp and grits in the South is served for breakfast, brunch, lunch, and dinner and is the breakfast staple for shrimp fishermen in the Carolinas. The "grits belt" seems to stretch from Louisiana through the South to the Carolinas. A customer who vacations a lot on the west coast of Florida introduced raspberries and grits to me. This dish is served for breakfast in many of the local diners and restaurants as you approach South Georgia, Alabama, and northern Florida. For me, it's a new way to enjoy two of my favorite foods.

½ pint fresh or frozen raspberries

¼ cup sugar

3⅓ cups cooked grits, about 1 cup dry

In a small bowl combine the raspberries and sugar. Cover the bowl and refrigerate overnight to break down the berries and form a syrup.

Cook the grits according to the package instructions. Spoon sugared raspberries over the warm grits and serve.

Makes 4 servings

NOTE: Stir the raspberries into the grits before eating, adding more sugar to taste.

EXTRAORDINARY EMPLOYEE

If a business owner is very blessed, he or she will have at least one invaluable person on the team. Pam Addicks is that blessing at Gabriel's. Neither one of us can remember when she actually came to work. I'm sure if we delved into it further, comparing dates and years, we would come up with an approximate time. Pam is not one to waste time doing something like that. She's more likely to be researching the next weekend's weddings or making sure the display case is just to her liking.

Pam's mother gave her the perfect background to be at Gabriel's. Her mom catered many weddings in Atlanta, preparing all the food, the wedding cake, the sugar flowers that decorated the cake, the punch . . . even the handmade mints that no Southern wedding was complete without. Pam remembers polishing a lot of silver, and their dining room table was usually covered with handmade sugar flowers. The cake topper of flowers that her mother made for Pam's wedding cake in 1976 is intact in her china cabinet to remind her of her mother's talent and hard work.

Tireless hard work is the only way to describe Pam's work ethic. We share the belief that we won't be in business long if we don't provide good customer care, quality products, and a friendly atmosphere.

Pam is not only a tireless business associate, she is also one of my best friends. She is an inspiration and example of selfless care of others. We have shared many December late nights of work, anxious moments about business, stories of our families, and laughter, at ourselves and, I must confess, at others along the way. I have seen many people come and go and am thankful that Pam is still my associate and my friend.

One winter Friday night, probably six or seven years ago, we had a wedding cake delivery into Atlanta. The florist had brought the fresh flower wedding cake topper by to us to deliver with the wedding cake. Pam and I, along with Michael

Wall, who was our pastry chef at that time, knew the area where this reception was to take place. The facility was very nicely done inside but had been converted from some sort of manufacturing plant to a special event facility and was located in a really dark, remote industrial part of Atlanta.

Michael is probably one of the kindest, most talented chefs we ever employed, and being the gentleman, he volunteered to venture into this area and deliver the cake to Atlanta around 5:00 PM, just before he would be leaving to go home to Cartersville, thirty-five miles north of Marietta.

Around 7:00 PM and just before the reception would be beginning for this bride and groom, we discovered that we failed to send the flowers along with the cake. What's a cake without the flowers for the top? It was cold and dark and Mike was already at home. I shuddered to think of driving into this industrial area alone, but there was nothing else to do but deliver the flowers.

Pam wouldn't hear of my going alone, so we jumped into my white Explorer with a wedding cake topper that would have to be put on the cake after the guests had already arrived. Neither one of us thought about our stained work clothes.

After finding the facility (it was just as dark and remote as we thought it would be), we relaxed a bit and even laughed that an off-duty policeman was outside. We entered the front door, only to find that the guests were indeed already there and in black tie. We were in soiled chef pants and shirts. There was no way I was walking into that reception looking like I did with a little arrangement of flowers.

We decided to try to find the kitchen and ask one of the catering staff to put the flowers on the cake. On the opposite side of a very dark office I saw a light and surmised that it must be the kitchen. Pam was concerned about walking through this dark office to the other side of the room to some place that we weren't even sure was the kitchen. But the room full of elegantly dressed guests was more intimidating than some dark office. I swung open the glass door, with Pam practically walking up my back she was so close behind me. I safely made it about five or six steps into the room before I heard this very deep growl and two big golden eyes popped up to about 3 feet high off the ground. Pam got the message also, and we both spun on a dime and flew back out the way we came with the dog barking like crazy. I nearly ran over my dear faithful friend, who so kindly accompanied me on this errand.

To this day, neither one of us can remember how we got those flowers on the cake. I think we finally found a waitstaff person wandering around and asked him to take care of it. I just remember shaking so hard my teeth were chattering. We loaded our shaking selves back into the car and headed to Marietta. We weren't a mile up the road before we were laughing so hard and commenting that this adventure would be one to recall in years to come.

Here we are years later, and if you ask Pam, she'll tell you that she's still having to take care of me . . . oh, am I ever so thankful for her!

Pam Addicks

SANDWICHES AND SALADS

From Pimento Cheese to Ambrosia

Mama's Pimento Cheese

My mother and grandmother made this all of my life. Dad was not happy when there was none in the refrigerator. This is the pimento cheese that we serve at Gabriel's.

¾	cup mayonnaise	1	(2-ounce) jar diced pimentos, well drained
1	teaspoon sugar		
2	cups (8 ounces) grated mild Cheddar cheese		

In a medium bowl whisk the mayonnaise and the sugar. Add the cheese and the pimento, combining well. If necessary, add a little more mayonnaise for spreading consistency after refrigeration. Spread on bread for a luncheon treat or serve with crackers as an appetizer.

Makes 2 to 2½ cups

Alternatives or additions:
- Use half mild and half sharp Cheddar cheese.
- Grill pimento cheese sandwich so the cheese melts.
- Cook and chop three to four pieces bacon and add to the mixture.
- Add ⅓ cup toasted chopped pecans.
- When making a sandwich, add a slice of tomato or a couple of slices of bacon or both.

Turkey and Ham Stacker

This is one of our best-selling sandwiches at the store. Men invariably love it.

2	slices wheat, sourdough, or 9-grain bread
	Mustard, to taste
	Mayonnaise, to taste
3	ounces sliced ham
3	ounces sliced turkey
2	slices cooked bacon
1	ounce sliced provolone, Swiss, or Cheddar cheese
2	slices fresh tomato
	Lettuce

Spread the bread slices with the mustard and mayonnaise. Stack the meats, bacon, and cheese on the bread. Top with tomato and lettuce.

Makes 1 serving

Mama's Pimento Cheese (page 44)

TUNA SALAD

Gabriel's uses this recipe for tuna sandwiches and our tuna scoop salad. We serve our salad with cheese straws and a wedge of apple.

4	hard-boiled eggs, peeled and chopped	⅓	cup mayonnaise
1	(9-ounce) can tuna, drained	¼	teaspoon lemon-pepper seasoning
1	cup chopped celery	¼	teaspoon salt
¼	cup chopped green onion	3	drops Tabasco sauce
¼	cup sweet pickle relish		

In a medium bowl mix the egg, tuna, celery, onion, and relish. In a small bowl mix the mayonnaise, the lemon-pepper seasoning, salt, and Tabasco, combining well. Spoon the mayonnaise mixture over the tuna and combine all the ingredients. Chill until ready to serve.

Makes 4 to 6 servings

Chicken Salad from Gabriel's

This is the chicken salad that we serve at the restaurant. We roast between 80 and 100 pounds of chicken breasts each week to make it. Roasting, in our estimation, gives it a better flavor.

4	cups chopped cooked roasted chicken	1	tablespoon lemon juice
2	cups thinly sliced celery	½	teaspoon salt
¾	cup mayonnaise		White pepper, to taste
¼	cup whipping cream	1	cup red grapes, cut in half, or ½ cup
¼	cup sweet pickle relish		toasted slivered almonds
2	tablespoons minced onion		

In a large bowl combine the chicken and celery. In a small bowl whisk together the mayonnaise, whipping cream, sweet pickle relish, minced onion, lemon juice, salt, and white pepper. Toss the mayonnaise mixture with the chicken. Cover and chill. Add the grapes or almonds just before serving.

Makes 6 servings

RICH'S CHICKEN SALAD AMANDINE

An Atlanta newspaper reported that this is the famous chicken salad that was served for years in the Magnolia Room of Rich's, a well-known Atlanta downtown department store.

3½	pounds chicken breasts	1½	teaspoons white pepper
	Salt, to taste	2	cups mayonnaise
6	celery stalks, diced	½	cup toasted almond slices
½	cup pickle relish		

In a large stockpot boil the chicken breasts in lightly salted water until the meat is tender. Reserve the stock for future use. Allow the chicken to cool. Separate the meat from the bones and skin. Leave the chicken in medium-size strips.

In a medium bowl, fold the celery, pickle relish, and white pepper into the mayonnaise. Fold the chicken into the mayonnaise mixture. Cover and refrigerate. Garnish with almond slices before serving.

Makes 6 to 8 servings

WHITE MEAT CHICKEN SALAD

4	boneless, skinless chicken breast halves		White pepper, to taste
½	cup diced celery	½	cup toasted almonds or 1 cup seedless white grapes, cut in half
	Dash of white wine vinegar		Bibb lettuce leaves, washed and
1	cup mayonnaise		dried, or slices of fresh, ripened
½	cup heavy cream		avocado
	Salt, to taste		

In a large stockpot, boil the chicken breasts in salted water until the chicken is tender. Allow to cool. Chop the chicken into bite-size pieces and place in a large bowl. Add the celery.

In a small bowl whisk the vinegar and the mayonnaise. Add the heavy cream and whisk well. Combine the mayonnaise mixture with the chopped chicken. Add salt and white pepper, to taste. Stir in the toasted almonds or white grapes. Serve a scoop of chicken salad on a bed of lettuce leaves or on a bed of sliced avocado.

Makes 6 servings

SHRIMP SALAD

Dot Harrison, the mother of my good friend Howard Simpson, shared this recipe with me many years ago.

1	(1-pound) box macaroni shells		1	(6-ounce) jar pimentos, drained
1	tablespoon prepared mustard		2	medium Kosher dill pickles, chopped
1	cup mayonnaise		1	medium onion, chopped
1	tablespoon Spanish olive oil		½	cup chopped black olives
6	hard-boiled eggs, peeled and chopped			Garlic salt, to taste
3	to 5 pounds medium shrimp*, cooked and peeled			Salt and pepper, to taste

Cook the macaroni until tender according to the package directions. Drain and cool. In a small bowl whisk together the mustard, mayonnaise, and olive oil. In a large bowl combine the chopped eggs, macaroni, shrimp, pimentos, pickles, and onion. Add the mayonnaise mixture to the macaroni mixture and toss well. Season with garlic salt, salt, and pepper. Refrigerate until ready to serve.

Makes 8 to 10 servings

* If you use shrimp larger than medium, chop the shrimp into bite-size pieces.

SHRIMP AND AVOCADO SALAD

This salad is delicious when served with hot, sliced French bread and real butter.

3	cups cooked, deveined large shrimp	½	cup green pitted olives or stuffed pimento olives, sliced
1	small onion, diced		
½	cup olive oil	3	cups cooked instant rice
3	lemons, juiced		Red or green lettuce leaves
	Salt and pepper, to taste		Tomato wedges or peeled mango or pineapple slices, for garnish
3	tablespoons chopped cilantro		
2	large avocados, peeled and diced		

Cut each shrimp into three to four bite-size pieces. Place in a medium bowl. In a small bowl mix together the onion, olive oil, lemon juice, salt and pepper, and cilantro. Pour over the shrimp. Marinate at least 2 hours or overnight in the refrigerator.

Add the avocados, olives, and rice to the marinated shrimp. Mix well. Serve on a red or green lettuce leaf. Garnish the plate with a tomato wedge or a slice of fresh, peeled mango or pineapple.

Makes 4 to 6 servings

NOTE: Chopped, cooked chicken can be substituted for the shrimp.

HOT POTATO SALAD

8	medium baking potatoes	1	(10¾-ounce) can cream of chicken soup
⅓	cup chopped green onions	1	teaspoon Cavenders Greek seasoning
1	cup grated Cheddar cheese		Salt and pepper, to taste
1	pint sour cream	2	cups cornflakes
¾	cup (1½ sticks) butter or margarine, melted and divided		

Preheat the oven to 375 degrees. Place the potatoes on aluminum foil. Bake the potatoes 1 hour or until well done. Refrigerate overnight.

Peel and grate the potatoes. In a medium bowl mix the potatoes, green onion, grated cheese, and sour cream. In another medium bowl combine ½ cup of the melted butter, the cream of chicken soup, Greek seasoning, salt, and pepper. Stir into the potato mixture.

Preheat the oven to 325 degrees. Coat a 13 x 9-inch baking dish with nonstick cooking spray. Spread the potato mixture in the prepared dish. Mix the cornflakes and the remaining ¼ cup butter in a zip-top bag and crush. Top the potatoes with the crushed cornflake mixture. Bake for 30 minutes, or until the mixture bubbles. This can be prepared ahead of time and frozen.

Makes 10 to 12 servings

WARM SWEET POTATO SALAD

A recipe from Executive Chef Thomas McEachern of Rays on the River, Atlanta

3	large sweet potatoes		Salt and pepper, to taste
3	large Idaho (or russet) potatoes	1½	cups extra-virgin olive oil
2	shallots, minced	6	tablespoons chopped fresh parsley
½	cup balsamic vinegar	4	tablespoons capers
½	cup grain mustard		

Place the sweet potatoes and the Idaho potatoes in a pot with salted water to cover. Bring the water to a boil and cook the potatoes until tender when pierced with a fork. Drain and cool the potatoes. Peel and cut them into thick wedges. Place in a large bowl.

In a medium bowl whisk together the shallots, vinegar, mustard, salt, and pepper. Gradually whisk in the olive oil and continue to whisk until fully emulsified. Add the parsley and capers to the potatoes and just enough of the vinaigrette to coat the potatoes liberally. Add extra vinaigrette as needed.

Makes 16 servings

Aggie's Macaroni Salad

This recipe is from my Greek friend Aggie Moraitakis. I first served it at my daughter Stephanie's graduation from Furman University. We serve it now every day at Gabriel's.

Dressing
½	cup salad oil
1	tablespoon plus 1 teaspoon lemon juice
1	tablespoon plus 1 teaspoon white wine vinegar
2	teaspoons dried oregano
2	teaspoons salt
¼	teaspoon black pepper

Salad
1	(16-ounce) package elbow or twisted macaroni
	Cavender's Greek seasoning, to taste
2	tablespoons chopped fresh dill
1	cup chopped green bell pepper
½	cup thinly sliced green onions
1	(16-ounce) container sliced fresh mushrooms
1	large tomato, chopped
½	to ¾ pound feta cheese
1	(14-ounce) can garbanzo beans, drained
½	cup chopped black pitted olives

Prepare the dressing in a small bowl. Whisk together the salad oil, lemon juice, vinegar, oregano, salt, and black pepper until emulsified.

Prepare the salad. Cook the macaroni according to the package directions, draining off the water. Place the macaroni in a large bowl and cover with the dressing while the pasta is still hot. Allow the pasta to cool. Add Greek seasoning, the fresh dill, bell pepper, and onions. Stir to mix. Cover and store in the refrigerator until ready to serve.

Just before serving, add the mushrooms, tomato, feta cheese, garbanzo beans, and black olives, tossing gently.

Makes 12 servings

SUMI SALAD

This delicious Asian-flavored coleslaw comes from my friend Marcelle David. At Gabriel's we modify this recipe to serve the slaw on our low-carb turkey Reuben wrap. Using a store-bought, low-carb wrap, a store-bought, no-carb/no-calorie Thousand Island dressing, we fill the wrap with three to four ounces of turkey and a good scoop of this coleslaw made with a sugar substitute equal to the four tablespoons sugar.

8 tablespoons sesame seeds	1 (6-ounce) package rice-flour noodles
8 tablespoons slivered almonds	4 tablespoons sugar
1 tablespoon plus ¾ cup vegetable oil, divided	1 teaspoon salt
	1 teaspoon ground pepper
½ head cabbage, shredded	6 tablespoons rice vinegar
4 green onions, sliced in thin rings	

In a small skillet brown the sesame seeds and almonds in 1 tablespoon of the oil over medium heat. Set aside. In a large bowl combine the cabbage and onions. Crumble the rice noodles into the cabbage mixture. In a small bowl combine the remaining ¾ cup of the oil, the sugar, salt, pepper, and rice vinegar to make a dressing. Pour the dressing over the cabbage mixture and toss well. Add the sesame seeds and almonds just prior to serving.

Makes 6 servings

TIP: Find a grocer who sells sesame seeds in bulk because they are costly in the small jars in the spice section.

RICE, TOMATO, AND BLACK BEAN SALAD

2⅔ cups canned low-sodium chicken broth
1⅓ cups Basmati rice
1 (16-ounce) can black beans, drained and rinsed
¾ pound plum tomatoes, seeded and chopped
1 green bell pepper, chopped
1 cup chopped sweet onion
¼ cup balsamic vinegar
3 tablespoons olive oil
2 tablespoons chopped fresh basil or 2 teaspoons dried
1 tablespoon chopped fresh garlic or the equivalent of minced garlic in water
Salt and pepper, to taste

In a heavy saucepan bring the chicken broth and the rice to a boil over medium-high heat, stirring occasionally. Reduce the heat to low and cook, covered, about 20 minutes or until the broth is absorbed. Spoon the rice into a large bowl and cool 15 minutes. Add the black beans, tomatoes, bell pepper, and onion.

In a small bowl whisk together the vinegar, olive oil, basil, and garlic to make a dressing. Add the dressing to the salad and toss lightly to coat the rice and vegetables. Season with salt and pepper, to taste. Serve warm or at room temperature.

Makes 8 servings

Gabriel's Coleslaw

Southerners love coleslaw with almost any kind of cooked beans.

1	large green cabbage, cored and shredded	¼	cup sugar
2	medium carrots, shredded	¼	cup mayonnaise
½	sweet onion, chopped	1	tablespoon salt
½	red bell pepper, chopped	¼	cup cider or red wine vinegar

In a large bowl mix the cabbage, carrots, onion, and bell pepper. In a small bowl whisk together the sugar, mayonnaise, salt, and vinegar until the sugar is dissolved to make a dressing. Pour the dressing over the cabbage mixture, stirring well to coat the cabbage. Refrigerate until ready to serve.

Makes 8 servings

NOTE: Many of our customers at Gabriel's don't like onion in the coleslaw so we leave it out. I like sweet onion in most everything, so I use it when I make coleslaw at home.

Spinach Salad with Apples and Gorgonzola Cheese

This recipe is from Gail Ré, who is not only my dear friend of many years but also a very talented artist. Some of her drawings hang in my home and one in my store is a gift from her. Gail has decorated Gabriel's Desserts twice for me now. You'll see her touch not only in two drawings on the walls but from the floor to the ceiling in paint color and style. Customers comment often on the warmth they feel from the décor when they come in. I'm so grateful to friends like Gail and loyal customers who have given so much of themselves to make Gabriel's successful.

2	bags baby spinach	1/2	cup olive oil
1	Golden Delicious or Granny Smith apple	1/2	cup white vinegar
1/2	red onion	2	packages sugar substitute
1/2	cup firmly packed dark brown sugar	6	ounces Gorgonzola cheese, divided
1	cup chopped pecans		

Wash the spinach and place in a large bowl. Core the apple and thinly slice it. Then cut the slices in half. Add to the spinach. Thinly slice the onion and cut the slices in half. Add to the spinach.

In a small skillet carefully melt the brown sugar over medium heat. Add the pecans and stir to coat them with the liquefied sugar. Remove the pecans from the heat and let cool.

In a small bowl or a salad dressing jar, mix the olive oil, vinegar, and sugar substitute, shaking or whisking well to combine all ingredients to make a dressing. Add 2 ounces of the Gorgonzola cheese to the dressing.

When ready to serve add the pecans to the spinach, along with the remaining Gorgonzola cheese. Top with the dressing and toss to coat well.

Makes 6 to 8 servings

TIP: Caramelized nuts are so tasty in most green salads. They can be prepared ahead and stored in an airtight container at room temperature for a week or so.

CRUNCHY ROMAINE TOSS WITH FRESH RASPBERRIES

This is probably my favorite salad.

4	tablespoons unsalted butter	1	cup sugar
1	cup walnut pieces	1	cup salad oil
1	(3-ounce) package regular-flavor Ramen noodles	½	cup wine vinegar or balsamic vinegar
1	head fresh broccoli florets	3	teaspoons soy sauce
1	head romaine lettuce		Salt and pepper, to taste
4	green onions		
1	(10-ounce) package frozen raspberries, or 1 (12-ounce) package fresh		

In a medium skillet melt the butter over medium heat. Add the walnuts and the Ramen noodles and brown in the butter. Let cool on paper towels.

Wash the broccoli and cut into bite-size pieces. Wash the romaine and break into bite-size pieces. Chop the green onions into small rings. If the raspberries are frozen, thaw and drain before using. In a large salad bowl combine the noodles, walnuts, broccoli, romaine, onions, and raspberries. In a small bowl whisk together the sugar, oil, vinegar, and soy sauce until the sugar is dissolved to make a dressing. Pour the dressing over the salad in the bowl and toss well. Serve immediately.

Makes 4 to 6 servings

Artichoke Tomato Salad with Feta Cheese Dressing

2 medium tomatoes, cubed

4 green onions, thinly sliced

1 small cucumber, cubed into ½-inch pieces

1 (14-ounce) can artichoke hearts, drained and quartered

¼ cup chopped red bell pepper

¼ cup pitted ripe olives, halved

¼ cup plus 2 tablespoons olive oil

2 tablespoons lemon juice

½ cup crumbled feta cheese

1 teaspoon fresh parsley

½ teaspoon coriander

¼ teaspoon freshly ground black pepper

3 cups shredded iceberg lettuce

In a large bowl combine the tomatoes, onions, cucumber, artichokes, bell pepper, and olives. In a small bowl whisk together the olive oil, lemon juice, feta cheese, parsley, coriander, and black pepper to make a dressing. Pour the feta cheese dressing over the vegetables and marinate 2 to 3 hours. At serving time, add the marinated vegetables to the lettuce, tossing gently.

Makes 6 to 8 servings

TOMATO, ARTICHOKE, AND BREAD SALAD

2	(6-ounce) jars marinated artichoke hearts, drained	2	teaspoons honey
¼	cup balsamic vinegar	5	tablespoons mayonnaise
2	tablespoons chopped green onion tops	½	cup extra-virgin olive oil
1	tablespoon fresh lemon juice	1	small red onion, thinly sliced
1	tablespoon coarse-grain Dijon mustard	2	cups cherry tomatoes, halved
		2	cups day-old bread cubes
			Parmesan cheese, freshly grated

In a food processor chop 1 jar of the artichoke hearts. Add the vinegar, onion tops, lemon juice, mustard, and honey. Pour the mixture into a medium bowl. Add the mayonnaise, whisking until smooth. Whisk in the olive oil to make a dressing. Cover and chill the dressing for at least 30 minutes. (The dressing will keep about seven days if covered and refrigerated.)

When ready to serve, combine the remaining jar of artichoke hearts, the onion slices, tomato, and bread cubes. Toss with your favorite dressing and top with a heavy coating of grated Parmesan.

Makes 6 servings

MINTED TOMATO AND CUCUMBER RELISH

1/2	cup canned chickpeas, drained	1 1/2	tablespoons red pepper flakes
1	large red onion, diced	2	tablespoons ground cumin
5	cucumbers, diced	1/4	cup minced garlic
12	tomatoes, seeded and diced	1/4	cup minced shallots
1/2	cup chopped mint leaves	1 1/2	tablespoons lemon zest
1/4	cup chopped lemon basil or regular basil	1	cup olive oil
1/2	cup rice wine vinegar		Salt and pepper, to taste

In a large bowl combine the chickpeas, onion, cucumbers, tomatoes, mint, and lemon basil. Gently stir in the vinegar, red pepper flakes, cumin, garlic, shallots, lemon zest, and olive oil. Season with salt and pepper, to taste.

Makes 10 servings

NOTE: This relish accompanies any fish, pork, beef, or fresh crab. Or serve it with shrimp for a tasty seafood cocktail.

Apple, Cranberry, and Blue Cheese Salad

Served daily at Gabriel's, this salad is a favorite.

Honey Balsamic Salad Dressing

4	shallots, minced
4	cloves garlic, minced
1	cup balsamic vinegar
3	ounces honey
3	ounces Dijon mustard
½	teaspoon salt
½	teaspoon black pepper
2	cups olive oil

Salad

1	head red leaf lettuce
1	to 2 heads Bibb lettuce
1	cup pecans
½	cup firmly packed light brown sugar
1	to 2 Granny Smith apples, sliced wafer thin
½	cup craisins (dried cranberries)
½	cup blue cheese crumbles

Prepare the dressing. In a medium bowl whisk together the shallots, garlic, vinegar, honey, mustard, salt, and pepper. Slowly whisk in the oil, combining well. Store in the refrigerator until ready to use.

For the salad, wash and dry the greens and set aside. Put the pecans in a medium skillet over medium heat and add the sugar. Stir constantly until the sugar is completely melted and the pecans are coated. Wash and core the apples, cut into fourths, and slice thinly into bite-size pieces. In a large bowl, combine the greens, craisins, apples, and blue cheese crumbles. Just before serving, top with enough of the dressing to lightly coat the salad when tossed. Sprinkle with the pecans.

Makes 4 to 6 servings

TIP: You can prepare apple slices ahead by placing them in a small zip-top plastic bag. Squeeze the juice of a fresh lemon over them. Close the bag and refrigerate until ready to use.

BROCCOLI AND RAISIN SALAD

We serve this at Gabriel's without the sunflower seeds.

6	cups broccoli florets, washed and chopped into bite-size pieces	1/3	cup sugar
1/2	cup raisins	2	tablespoons white vinegar
1/2	sweet onion, chopped	6	slices bacon, cooked and chopped
1	cup mayonnaise	1/2	cup shelled sunflower seeds (optional)

In a large bowl combine the broccoli, raisins, and onion. In a small bowl, whisk together the mayonnaise, sugar, and vinegar until the sugar dissolves. Toss the mayonnaise mixture with the broccoli mixture. Chill for at least two hours. Add the bacon and the sunflower seeds, if desired, just before serving.

Makes 4 to 6 servings

Apple, Cranberry, and Blue Cheese Salad (page 64)

CRANBERRY CHUTNEY

This chutney will keep in the refrigerator for about two weeks. Serve small amounts with roasted chicken and vegetables or turkey and cornbread dressing. Or spread lightly on roasted chicken or turkey sandwiches.

1	pound fresh cranberries	1/2	teaspoon ground cloves
1	cup sugar	1/4	teaspoon ground allspice
1/2	cup firmly packed brown sugar	1	cup water
1/2	cup golden raisins	1	cup chopped onion
2	teaspoons ground cinnamon	1	cup chopped Granny Smith apple
1 1/2	teaspoons ground ginger		

In a large saucepan combine the cranberries, sugar, brown sugar, and raisins. Cook over medium heat for about 15 minutes, stirring often. (The juice will be released from the cranberries.) In a small bowl combine the cinnamon, ginger, cloves, and allspice. Stir into the cranberry mixture. Add the water, onion, and apple. Reduce the heat and simmer, uncovered, stirring occasionally, for about 15 minutes or until thickened. Let the mixture cool to room temperature before storing in an airtight container. Serve cold.

Makes 1 quart (4 cups)

CRANBERRY SALAD

This salad was served at a Walker School Christmas luncheon at least twenty-five or thirty years ago. I have kept the recipe all these years because it was so delicious.

1	cup chopped fresh cranberries	1/2	cup diced celery
3/4	cup sugar, divided	1/2	cup chopped walnuts
1	(3-ounce) package cherry gelatin		Bibb lettuce leaves
1	cup hot water		Walnut halves, a few fresh
1	cup cold water		cranberries and/or fresh cherries for
3/4	cup diced apple		garnish (optional)

In a small bowl combine the cranberries with 1/2 cup of the sugar and let stand for several hours or overnight.

In another small bowl, dissolve the gelatin and the remaining 1/4 cup sugar with the hot water. Stir in the cold water. Allow the gelatin to set in the refrigerator until it begins to thicken. Stir in the cranberries, apple, celery, and walnuts. Pour into a salad mold that has been sprayed lightly with nonstick cooking spray. Cover the mold tightly with plastic wrap, or put the cover on the mold if it has one. Refrigerate for at least 4 hours or overnight to allow salad to congeal.

When ready to serve, garnish the outside edge of a serving plate with the lettuce leaves. Fill a bowl 2 to 3 inches wider than the mold with hot tap water. Run a thin knife around the top inside edge of the mold between the mold and the salad to help release the salad. Dip the bottom side of the mold into the hot water for 10 to 15 seconds and invert onto the lettuce-lined serving plate. If the salad doesn't release, gently tap the sides and bottom of the mold or dip the mold back into the hot water for a few more seconds and then invert onto the serving plate. Garnish the salad with the walnut halves, fresh cranberries, or cherries, if desired.

Makes 10 to 12 servings

FRESH AMBROSIA

My grandmother, Mommie (Charlye Ethyl Paul Heath), who was my mother's mom, prepared this dish when we all gathered for holidays. It is nothing but fresh peeled and sectioned delicious fruit but was a total labor of love. Mommie sat at the end of my mother's kitchen table, peeled fruit, and giggled for hours. Now that both Mother and Mommie are gone, my girls look for the ambrosia on holidays and know that I will perform that labor of love. Some things are just worth the effort.

1   bag navel oranges
1   bag grapefruit, pink if possible, as they are more colorful
1   large fresh pineapple, peeled, cored, and chopped, or 1 (20-ounce) can chunks in pineapple juice

1   small jar maraschino cherries, drained and cut in halves (optional)
1   (3½-ounce) can flaked coconut (optional)
1   cup chopped pecans (optional)
     Sliced bananas (optional)

Peel the oranges, removing most of the pith (the white lining under the skin). Over a large bowl, section the oranges, removing the membranes, any remaining pith, and the seeds, retaining all of the pulp and juice. Repeat the process for the grapefruit, mixing the fruit sections together. Add the pineapple, including any juice. Stir well to blend the fruits and the juices. Cover the bowl and refrigerate until ready to serve.

If desired, add the cherries, coconut, pecans, and bananas before serving.

Makes various quantities depending on the size of bags of fruit that you purchase.

NOTE: The optional ingredients can be served in small bowls so family and guests can add what they want. Also, the bananas, coconut, and pecans will soften if you have leftovers, so I like to store the oranges, grapefruit, and pineapple separately. This trio will easily keep three days in the refrigerator.

TIP: Your best friend when preparing this type recipe is a good sharp knife. I use a fillet knife because the blade is long and narrow. The knife is lightweight and very sharp.

Strawberry Almond Salad

My friend Jane Stacey shares one of the best salads you'll ever eat.

1	(3-ounce) package Ramen noodles, finely crushed	2	tablespoons soy sauce
7	tablespoons butter, divided	1/2	teaspoon black pepper
1	cup sliced almonds	2	different bunches of lettuce, red leaf, green leaf, or romaine, washed and dried
1/2	cup sesame seeds		
1	cup olive oil	1	quart fresh strawberries, washed, dried, and sliced
1	cup sugar		
1/2	cup white vinegar	1/2	cup dried cranberries

In a medium skillet sauté the crushed noodles in 3 tablespoons of the butter over medium heat. Drain on paper towels and set aside. In the same skillet over medium heat, sauté the almonds in 2 tablespoons of the butter. Drain on paper towels and set aside. Melt the remaining 2 tablespoons of butter in the skillet and sauté the sesame seeds. Stir often until toasted and browned. Drain on paper towels and set aside.

In a medium microwave-safe bowl, whisk together the olive oil, sugar, and vinegar, stirring vigorously. Microwave for 30 seconds. Stir well. Whisk in the soy sauce and black pepper. In a large salad bowl combine the two lettuces, the strawberries, and the cranberries. Refrigerate if not serving immediately. Just before serving, add the noodles, almonds, and sesame seeds. Toss with the dressing and serve immediately.

Makes 6 to 8 servings

RICH'S FROZEN FRUIT SALAD

Many people who grew up in Georgia have vivid memories of the heyday of Rich's department store. A local newspaper shared the famous Frozen Fruit Salad served in Rich's Magnolia Room in downtown Atlanta.

1	(8-ounce) package cream cheese, softened
½	cup confectioners' sugar
⅓	cup mayonnaise
2	teaspoons vanilla extract
1	(8¾-ounce) can sliced peaches, well drained
½	cup maraschino cherry halves, well drained

1	(30-ounce) can fruit cocktail, well drained
1	(6½-ounce) can crushed pineapple, well drained
2	cups miniature marshmallows
½	cup whipping cream, whipped
	A few drops food coloring, if desired

Combine the cream cheese and confectioners' sugar in a mixing bowl. Add the mayonnaise, mixing well. Add the vanilla extract. Fold in the fruit and the marshmallows. Gently fold the whipped cream into the fruit mixture. Add the food coloring, if desired. Ladle into large, paper soufflé cups or muffin liners. Freeze immediately.

Defrost 15 minutes before serving. Do not allow the fruit to get soft. Remove the soufflé cups or muffin liners before serving.

Makes 12 servings

LEARNING THE ROPES—WITH FRIENDS BY YOUR SIDE

Once you take out a loan to start your business, things take a serious turn. There's no walking away unless you can write a check to repay the lending institution. Therefore, we had to make this endeavor work. We found a whole new meaning to the phrase "on the job training." Thank the Lord for good employees and good friends.

The four or five Christmas seasons that we baked out of the house, we employed college students. Rand Elliott was our lead baker at home and also for the first Christmas we were in the retail store.

Our bakers at the retail store initially came from other home bakers just like me who wanted an opportunity to earn a few dollars. These initial bakers were great choices and stood the test of time for many of the first years. One of them, Lydia DeBuyser, had been my mother's daytime caregiver when Mother lived with Ed and me because of her dementia. She loved Mother but was somewhat burned out with nursing and suffering and gave baking a try. She was an excellent baker.

Maria Geros, a longtime friend and member of my "Birthday Club," came to bake at the store when Stephanie, my oldest daughter, was expecting her first child and lived in Gig Harbor, Wash. I knew Maria was a good cook, and she was my "kitchen pass" from Ed to allow me to be gone for two weeks and still keep the cakes coming out of the oven at Gabriel's. Maria is probably one of the best and fastest untrained bakers I have ever seen. She and Lydia were so efficient they hardly needed me to bake when I returned two weeks later. They both did, however, need me on the weekends. They didn't like to work on Saturdays.

It was apparent that to help the business grow we had to have professional pastry chefs, cooks, and cake decorators to handle the potential business for a product such as ours. I learned that it was smarter to hire someone who

worked faster and was more talented and trained than I. That was hard for me; I wanted to have my hands in everything.

With the addition of special-occasion and wedding cakes, fancy little individual desserts, and a larger variety of cakes, I needed help. We had begun with recipes for six to eight cakes, a brownie or two, and lemon squares.

Along with professionals, we also hired someone to wash dishes and clean after the close of business. The pros showed me where to spend my energy and benefit the growth of the business most. Michael Wall, Jean Luc Verbist, and Sue Siemens all surface in my mind as huge contributors of talent to Gabriel's over the years.

It also became apparent that a 650- to 750-square-foot store, sitting perpendicular to the street, could not attract the volume of business that was needed to support the caliber of staff that was required for the quality of product that was in demand in our area. Birthday cakes, wedding cakes, and desserts on weekends were not enough.

After struggling and searching for answers (and cash flow), I saw a business model that seemed to work—a bakery and a deli. A daily cash flow from a lunch crowd is what I needed.

Eventually, the space next door to our bakeshop became available and we literally knocked two holes in the wall, installed a walk-in cooler and freezer, a small kitchen area and started offering soups and salads and desserts. The reception of the community of a new place for lunch was good, but we had only twenty seats inside and about six seats outside in good weather. Once again I had hired a great staff but not enough space or exposure to support it.

One day I realized there was no good place to get cornbread and Southern vegetables. Cynthia Robinson was and still is our savory chef; she, being the natural Southern cook that she is, and Theresa Turner, jumped right in, and we started offering four vegetables and cornbread along with the sandwiches and soup at lunchtime. It was a big day when we served forty-eight vegetable plates from our little four-portion steam table. For three years Cynthia and Theresa made the soups, salads, vegetables, and cornbread in a little tiny kitchen with the help of a couple of part-time employees. They're both still cooking in the new store but with a staff of eight.

Along the way, we have had and still have, talented decorators and kitchen managers to grow the business—Pam Addicks, Jennifer Dauphin, Aisha Cheeks, Roland Garcia, Mo Bednardowski . . . all hardworking, talented, and

dedicated. To present consistent, quality product, you must assemble a team with those same characteristics: quality and consistency with a seriousness of purpose and very little tolerance in them for lesser effort from the rest of the staff. Along the way, we have worked hard, developed love and respect for each other, argued some, and have some good laughs. I'm not saying we're "there" yet; we can never quit learning and growing. I can say we are "seasoned."

Along with a good staff, I have had friends who have also helped Gabriel's grow. Besides Maria, there have been friends who pitched in when my family needed me. Trish Elliott worked one evening in the store with her daughter, Rand, when I was away for my grandson Wyatt's birth. She remembers trying to make caramel frosting (a tough task for a veteran), but I think even more traumatic was having to wear one of the really ugly hairnets.

When Mother died, my friends Marshall and Cindy Dye pitched in. Cindy made cream cheese frosting using a twenty-quart commercial mixer for the first time and blew six pounds of confectioners' sugar all over her. Marshall was delivering cakes for me on the day of Mother's funeral.

For a Christmas gift one year, my friend Elisha Shamblin delivered cakes to one of my commercial customers every day the week before Christmas because she knew we were busy and it would relieve me. Nancy Dorsey, a great organizer and a successful real estate salesperson, loves to work, for no pay, on Christmas Eve. She sees a lot of friends and neighbors who are our customers—and helps out a friend at the same time. Gail Ré, a longtime dear friend, decorated both the expanded old store and the new store we're in now. She even sewed the window treatments in the old store and brought in her neurologist husband, Peter, to hang them.

Then there's my friend, Carole Simpson, my most honest and loyal critic, and my biggest cheerleader. Through the years she has invited me to her beach house when I needed rest and tolerated my company when I was tired and troubled. My friend John Elliott was my landlord in my old store location. We were the anchor in that shopping center. When we learned we were going to be able to move to a building that was not under John's ownership, he was one of the first to call to congratulate me. There has truly been a group of devoted friends who have helped carry us on our journey. We would not have made it this far without them!

SOUPS
AND CHILIS

Mom's Comfort Foods

CHILLED CUCUMBER SOUP

My friend Dot Dunaway served this soup at the bridesmaids' luncheon for her daughter, Ann Dunaway Teh.

12	medium cucumbers
1²/₃	cups bread and butter pickles with the liquid
¹/₃	cup fresh dill, washed and picked from stem
2¹/₂	cups half-and-half

2¹/₂	cups plain yogurt
7	ounces sour cream
	Juice and zest of 1¹/₂ lemons
	Salt and pepper, to taste

Peel and seed the cucumbers. Cut them in half lengthwise. Chop them just enough to spin them in a blender. Slowly add the pickles and pickle juice as you blend the cucumbers. Fold in the dill after all of the cucumbers and pickles are pureed. Add the half-and-half, yogurt, sour cream, lemon juice and zest, and salt and pepper. Chill until ready to serve.

Makes 4 to 5 quarts (20–25 cups)

TOMATO BASIL SOUP

Every Monday, Gabriel's serves this as the soup of the day.

2	(28-ounce) cans Italian tomatoes		Salt and pepper, to taste
1	cup chicken broth	²⁄₃	cup heavy cream
1	tablespoon dried basil		

Pour the tomatoes into a 4-quart saucepan. Crush the tomatoes into small pieces using your hands. Add the chicken broth, basil, salt, and pepper. Bring the mixture to a boil and simmer over low heat for 20 to 30 minutes. Lower the heat and whisk in the heavy cream, heating thoroughly but not boiling.

Makes 6 to 8 servings

Black Bean Soup

1	pound dried black beans, cleaned and soaked overnight (or use the quick-soak method on the package)	1	large ham hock, with outer tough skin removed
6	cups water	¾	teaspoon ground cumin
4	cups chicken stock	2	tablespoons malt vinegar
1	bay leaf	1	teaspoon sugar
2	tablespoons olive oil	½	teaspoon salt
2	medium onions, finely diced	½	teaspoon pepper
2	garlic cloves, pressed or finely chopped	1	onion, finely diced (optional)
			Sour cream (optional)

In a strainer, rinse the beans with cold running water. In an 8-quart stockpot, combine the beans and the water. Be sure the water covers the beans. If not, add more until the beans are covered. Cover and bring to a boil over high heat. Reduce the heat and simmer for 2 hours, or until the beans are tender and can be mashed with a spoon. Remove 2 cups of the beans and 2 cups of the liquid and mash with a spoon until soft and pureed. Return the puree to the pot and add the chicken stock and bay leaf. Bring the soup to a simmer.

In a skillet, heat the olive oil over medium-high heat. Add the diced onions and the garlic, cooking until the onion is clear. Add the onion, garlic, ham hock, and cumin to the beans. Cover the pot and simmer 2 more hours. Add the vinegar, sugar, salt, and pepper. Simmer 15 minutes. Remove and discard the bay leaf. Remove the ham hock and cool. Chop the lean part of the hock into small pieces and return to the soup.

To serve, top bowls of hot soup with the finely diced onion and sour cream, if desired.

Makes 6 to 8 servings

LOADED BAKED POTATO SOUP

Gabriel's customers love this Thursday soup of the day.

4	large baking potatoes	1½	cups shredded Cheddar cheese, divided
⅔	cup butter or margarine		
⅔	cup all-purpose flour	12	slices bacon, cooked, crumbled, and divided
6	cups milk		
¾	teaspoon salt	4	green onions, chopped
½	teaspoon pepper	1	(8-ounce) carton sour cream

Preheat the oven to 400 degrees. Wash the potatoes. Place on aluminum foil, prick the skins several times with a fork and bake for approximately 1 hour. Cool and peel the potatoes. Cut the potatoes in half lengthwise and scoop out the pulp, setting it aside. Throw away the peeling.

In a 3- to 4-quart stockpot, melt the butter over medium heat. Add the flour and cook 2 minutes, stirring constantly so that the flour does not brown. Gradually add the milk, stirring constantly, and cook over medium heat until the mixture begins to thicken and boil. Reduce the heat to medium and stir in the potatoes, salt, pepper, 1 cup of the cheese, 1 cup of the bacon, and the green onions. Cook until the mixture is well heated but not boiling.

Just before serving, stir in the sour cream, combining thoroughly, and heat until hot but not boiling. Ladle into bowls and garnish with the remaining cheese and bacon.

Makes 6 to 8 servings

SHE-CRAB SOUP

This recipe was graciously given to us by The Charleston Crab House on Market Street in Charleston, South Carolina. It is one of the best we have ever eaten. Ed makes it when we really want to treat our guests or ourselves to something special.

2	tablespoons butter	1/2	tablespoon salt
2	tablespoons all-purpose flour	2	cups lump crabmeat
1	quart (4 cups) whole milk	5	drops onion juice
1/2	cup heavy cream	1/4	teaspoon mace
1/4	teaspoon white pepper	4	tablespoons sherry
1	lemon rind, grated		

In a heavy saucepan melt the butter over medium-high heat. Whisk in the flour and cook until the flour starts to turn light brown. Whisk in the milk, heavy cream, white pepper, lemon rind, salt, crabmeat, onion juice, and mace. Bring to a light boil, stirring often. Then reduce the heat to low. Simmer 15 to 20 minutes, stirring occasionally.

When ready to serve, ladle the soup into bowls and add a half-tablespoon sherry to each bowl.

Makes 8 servings

Fresh Minestrone Soup

Minestrone is supposed to be the Italian's meatless, inexpensive soup. To accomplish the same task, Southerners of the past cleaned out their refrigerator of leftover fresh vegetables. To cut cost, omit the marinated artichoke hearts in this recipe.

2	tablespoons olive oil		1	(8-ounce) can stewed tomatoes
4	carrots, sliced		1	(6-ounce) jar artichoke hearts, drained and chopped
2	small zucchini, sliced		1	large tomato, peeled, seeded, and chopped
1	onion, chopped			
1	large celery heart with leaves, chopped		1	small bunch spinach, washed and stems removed, or 1 (10-ounce) box frozen
1	teaspoon dried oregano			
1	teaspoon Greek seasoning		1	cup macaroni
2	garlic cloves, minced		2	tablespoons dried parsley
1	(8-ounce) package fresh mushrooms, sliced			Salt and pepper, to taste
2½	quarts (10 cups) chicken stock		½	cup Parmesan cheese, freshly grated
1	(8¾-ounce) can garbanzo beans, drained			

Heat the olive oil in a medium stockpot over medium-high heat. Add the carrots, zucchini, onion, celery, oregano, Greek seasoning, and garlic. Reduce the heat to low, cover, and let the vegetables simmer for 10 minutes. Add the mushrooms in the last two to three minutes. Add the chicken stock, garbanzo beans, stewed tomatoes, artichoke hearts, and fresh tomato. Simmer, covered, for 20 to 30 minutes. Add the spinach, macaroni, and parsley and simmer 10 minutes. Add salt and pepper, to taste. Ladle the soup into bowls, top with cheese, and serve immediately.

Makes 10 servings

SOUTHWESTERN CHICKEN SOUP

This is our most popular soup at Gabriel's. We serve it every day instead of rotating in once a week as we do the others. It is delicious, low fat, and healthy. My favorite accompaniment to this soup is one of our corn muffins . . . but there goes the low-fat aspect. The cornbread muffin recipe on can be found on page xxx.

1	tablespoon olive oil	⅛	teaspoon crushed red pepper
8	ounces boneless skinless chicken	1	(14-ounce) can chicken broth
	breasts, cut into ½-inch chunks	2	cups frozen whole kernel yellow corn
¼	cup diced onion	1	(14-ounce) can black beans, rinsed
2	cloves garlic, minced		and drained
1	teaspoon cumin	1	(14-ounce) can Mexican-style stewed
½	teaspoon salt		tomatoes
½	teaspoon chili powder		Chopped fresh cilantro, optional

In a Dutch oven or a 4-quart saucepan, heat the oil over medium heat. Add the chicken chunks and cook 3 to 4 minutes or until opaque. Add the onion, garlic, cumin, salt, chili powder, and red pepper, stirring frequently until the garlic and spices are fragrant. Stir in the chicken broth, corn, black beans, and tomatoes with juice. Bring to a boil over high heat. Reduce the heat, cover, and simmer 15 minutes. Ladle into bowls and top with fresh cilantro, if desired.

Makes 6 servings

Sausage, Corn and Bean Chowder

This is a good winter night supper served with bread and a salad.

1	pound ground sausage	1	(15-ounce) can white cannelloni
1	large onion, chopped		beans, drained
3	large potatoes, peeled and sliced	1	(15½-ounce) can cream-style corn
2	teaspoons salt	1	(15½-ounce) can whole kernel corn,
1	teaspoon basil		undrained
½	teaspoon white pepper	1	(12-ounce) can evaporated milk
2	cups water		

In a medium skillet crumble the sausage and brown over medium heat. Drain the fat, reserving 2 tablespoons. In a 4-quart stockpot, put the 2 tablespoons drippings, the browned sausage, and the onion. Sauté until the onion is clear. Add the potatoes, salt, basil, white pepper, water, and cannelloni beans. Simmer, covered, 15 minutes.

Stir in the corns, the corn liquid, and the evaporated milk. Cover and heat almost to boiling.

Makes 6 to 8 servings

Kielbasa and Tortellini Soup

2 tablespoons olive oil	10 cups canned low-salt chicken broth
4 cloves garlic, minced	4 cups fresh spinach
12 ounces smoked, cooked kielbasa sausage, sliced and cut into quarters	1 (15-ounce) can cannelloni beans, rinsed and drained
1 onion, chopped	1 (9-ounce) package fresh cheese-filled tortellini
1 cup fennel, chopped	
1½ tablespoons chopped fresh thyme	1 cup Parmesan or Asiago cheese, grated
¼ teaspoon crushed red pepper	

In a large stockpot heat the olive oil over medium heat. Add the garlic and sauté about 2 minutes. Add the sausage and sauté until browned. Add the onion, fennel, thyme, and red pepper. Cover the pot, reduce the heat to low, and sweat the vegetables for 10 to 15 minutes. Add the chicken broth and bring to a boil. Stir in the spinach and the beans. Lower the heat and cook until the spinach is wilted. Just before serving, add the tortellini and simmer about 5 minutes. Pasta should still be firm. Ladle into serving bowls and top with cheese.

Makes 6 to 8 servings

WHITE CHILI

My friend Nancy Bonds won the Chili Cookoff at First Baptist Church in Marietta several times with this recipe.

5	tablespoons olive oil	12	cups chicken stock
2	medium onions, diced	2	pounds cooked chicken, diced
4	large cloves garlic, minced	2	cups salsa, mild, medium or hot,
1	tablespoon ground cumin		or 1 (15-ounce) jar
1	teaspoon marjoram	1	to 2 cups shredded Mexican cheese,
1½	teaspoons oregano		or a mixture of 4 kinds cheese
1	tablespoon chopped jalapeños	1	(8-ounce) carton sour cream
½	teaspoon cayenne pepper		
1	pound dried Northern or navy beans		

In a large stockpot heat the olive oil, onion, garlic, cumin, marjoram, oregano, jalapeños, and cayenne pepper. Cook over medium heat for about 5 minutes. Add the dried beans and 10 to 12 cups chicken stock. Bring the mixture to a boil, reduce the heat, and simmer 3 hours. Taste the beans to make sure they are done. Add more stock if necessary. Add the chicken, salsa, and 1½ cups of the cheese.

When serving, sprinkle with the additional cheese and add a dollop of sour cream. This recipe freezes well.

Makes 4 quarts (20 cups)

NOTE: To make a lower fat, but very delicious version, don't add the cheese while cooking the soup. At Gabriel's we offer a generous ¼ cup of cheese on top of a 10-ounce bowl of chili if the customer requests it, along with a dollop of sour cream.

TIP: To cut the cooking time in half, you have two options: 1) Use the "quick-soak" method given on the bean packaging and add the beans after they have been soaked and then use only 10 cups of chicken stock, 2) Or substitute dried beans with 6 cups of canned Northern or navy beans, rinsed, and then use about 8 cups of stock.

BLACK BEAN TURKEY CHILI OVER RICE

This robust chili needs only a green side salad or a fresh fruit salad to make a whole meal. It's low fat and is just as good if you wish to leave the rice out of the recipe. It's a good serve-yourself meal for a casual gathering.

2	medium-size sweet onions	2	(4-ounce) cans chopped green chiles, drained
1	red bell pepper, finely chopped		
1	green bell pepper, finely chopped	2	cups chicken stock
6	cloves garlic, minced	3	tablespoons chili powder
3	tablespoons olive oil	1	tablespoon dried basil
2	pounds freshly ground turkey	1	tablespoon dried oregano
1	pound Italian turkey sausage, sliced	1	teaspoon salt
2	(16-ounce) cans black beans, drained	1/2	teaspoon pepper
1	(28-ounce) can Italian tomatoes, chopped and undrained	2	cups Basmati rice or brown rice
			Chopped fresh cilantro, to taste
1	(14-ounce) can Mexican style tomatoes, chopped and undrained	4	Roma tomatoes, chopped
1	(6-ounce) can tomato paste		

In a large stockpot, cook the onion, red bell pepper, green bell pepper, and garlic in 3 tablespoons olive oil over medium-high heat. Stir the vegetables. Reduce the heat to low and let the vegetables "sweat," covered, for 10 minutes or until tender. Add the ground turkey and sausage slices, cooking until the meats are browned and the turkey is crumbled. Drain well. Return the mixture to the stockpot, adding the black beans, the Italian and Mexican-style tomatoes, the tomato paste, chiles, chicken stock, chili powder, basil, oregano, salt, and pepper. Bring the mixture to a boil, reduce the heat, and simmer, covered, 30 minutes.

While the bean mixture is cooking, prepare the rice according to the package instructions. When done, mound 1/4 cup rice in the bottom of a soup bowl and ladle the chili over top when ready to serve. Garnish with cilantro and a tablespoon of chopped tomatoes.

Makes 8 servings

IN PURSUIT OF PERFECT RECIPES

When Gabriel's opened eleven years ago we made three "cooked" frostings—lemon cheese, caramel, and a 7-minute frosting. All three of these are used on old-fashioned Southern homemade cakes. The 7-minute frosting is not a problem; it's just time-consuming to stand at the stove for seven to eight minutes with a hand mixer, constantly cooking and beating. Spreading the frosting on the cake can be a little tricky too, but most cooks can learn to handle it.

The lemon cheese is really a curd. Southerners spread it between layers and on the top and sides of a yellow layer cake. It is delicious! Some of our customers then like a 7-minute frosting spread over the top and sides of the lemon cheese. Two cooked frostings can give a cake finisher a fit. The curd is time-consuming to cook, but the tricky part is keeping the cake stacked straight after it is spread with the frosting. My lemon cheese is Mary Moon's original recipe and one of my family's favorites. My first customer request for lemon cheese was from my good friend Madeline Knox for her son Jack's birthday. The Knoxes were my first victims of lemon cheese gone awry.

The cake was stacked perfectly when I put it in the box to deliver. But when it got to their home, the two top layers slid. If it weren't for the cake box, they would have been off the bottom layer completely. The secret to lemon cheese is giving the cake time to set up before moving—two or three hours, not 10 minutes like I probably gave it. Madeline graciously helped me straighten it and proceeded to serve it that night. How embarrassing when you're trying to become the next "Cake Lady."

Timing is not the case with cooked fudge and cooked caramel frostings. Plenty of time to "rest" on the cake without sliding is the case with those two also, but there is another key piece of knowledge: They need the right amount of time to cook the frosting and the right amount of time to beat the frosting after cooking. We spent two years at Gabriel's in pursuit of the answers.

We used candy thermometers (we still do on the caramel) costing from $3 to $40. We bought ice from the convenience store to set the mixing bowl in an ice bath, and we asked every customer we could if his or her grandmother or mother had made either, and if they had a recipe to share. I remember crying over caramel cakes sliding apart and the icing running off the cake onto the table and cooked fudge that never set up or set up too quickly. Every employee we had tried a hand at it.

One day, a good friend, Sue Fleming, sent me her grandmother's cooked fudge recipe. It worked, and we didn't have to put it in an ice bath (the ice never worked anyway). The key ingredient, I believe, is the corn syrup. It was not included in the other chocolate recipes.

We still use Mary Moon's caramel recipe. We got the cooking time and temperature right, finally figured out how long to beat it after cooking, and know it can be slightly reheated in the microwave to soften it. (All these tips are with the recipe in this book.) Savory cooking is an art, and you can "fudge" (no pun intended) on the ingredients, add or take away a pinch here and there, and little difference is made. Baking is chemistry and all ingredients must come together in the proper proportion or you have wasted time and money. Thanks to all of you who have shared recipes and tips with me over the years to change disasters into triumphs.

Hawaiian Rib-Eye Steak (page 95)

ENTRÉES

Meat & Two, Anyone?

Beef Tenderloin with Mushroom Sauce

The sauce is another good recipe from my friend Linda Cupp of Columbia, Missouri.

2	tablespoons olive oil	1	tablespoon soy sauce
1	(4- to 5-pound) beef tenderloin	1	(9-ounce) bottle Major Grey's
½	cup (1 stick) butter		chutney
1	pound sliced mushrooms		Salt and pepper, to taste
3	(10.5-ounce) cans mushroom sauce	½	cup dry sherry
1	tablespoon Worcestershire sauce		

Preheat the oven to 375 degrees. Heat the olive oil in a large skillet over medium-high. Brown the beef tenderloin on all sides in the hot oil. Place the tenderloin in a roasting pan. Bake for 20 to 25 minutes or until the internal temperature reaches 145 degrees for medium rare or 165 degress for medium well. Remove from the oven and let stand for 10 to 15 minutes.

In a medium saucepan, melt the butter over medium heat. Sauté the mushrooms until lightly browned. Add the cans of mushroom sauce, Worcestershire, soy sauce, chutney, and salt and pepper to taste. Bring to a boil. Add the sherry and simmer 5 minutes. Spread the sauce on top of the beef before serving, or serve the sauce on the side.

Makes 8 to 10 servings

Hawaiian Rib-Eye Steak

This is my husband Ed Gabriel's recipe. He is a grill master. You can search and may not find a better steak than he can grill. (See Ed's Grilling Tips on page 106.)

2	cups pineapple juice	½	teaspoon dry mustard
2½	ounces soy sauce	½	teaspoon garlic salt
2	ounces sherry	6	(½-pound) choice rib-eye steaks
1	cup firmly packed dark brown sugar, divided	1	(16-ounce) can sliced pineapple, drained

In a medium bowl, whisk together the pineapple juice, soy sauce, sherry, ³/₄ cup of the brown sugar, the dry mustard, and the garlic salt. Wash the steaks and pat dry with paper towels. Place them in a large zip-top bag and cover with the marinade. Marinate in the refrigerator for 36 to 48 hours.

Prepare the grill. Place the steaks over medium-high heat, turning and cooking to your desired degree of doneness. (Be attentive to steaks while grilling as the sugar in the marinade could cause high flare-ups. Reduce the temperature to a medium heat if flare-ups continue.) Sprinkle the remaining ¹/₄ cup brown sugar over the pineapple slices. Place on the grill, turning to brown on both sides. Serve a piece of pineapple on top of each hot steak.

Makes 6 servings

MARINATED BEEF KABOBS

Linda Cupp's family has been using her mother's marinade recipe for more than twenty-five years.

¼	cup soy sauce	3	yellow or zucchini squash, cut into 2-inch slices
½	cup vegetable oil		
2	tablespoons dark brown sugar	3	sweet onions, quartered
1½	tablespoons white sugar	3	red or green tomatoes, quartered
1	tablespoon vinegar	1	(16-ounce) package whole mushrooms
1	tablespoon ground ginger		
1	tablespoon garlic salt		Bacon strips (optional)
2	pounds sirloin beef chunks		

In a medium bowl, whisk together the soy sauce, oil, sugars, vinegar, ginger, and garlic salt. Pour into a zip-top bag. Add the beef chunks and refrigerate for at least two hours or overnight.

When ready to cook, heat the grill. Alternate the meat and vegetables on skewers. If desired, add a strip of bacon on the skewer between the meat and vegetables to add extra flavor. Grill the kabobs to desired doneness, occasionally basting skewers with the marinade.

Makes 4 to 6 servings

MEATLOAF THE FAMILY WILL LOVE

This is one of the two meats we serve daily at Gabriel's. It's a staple in our "meat-and-two" menu and makes a good meatloaf sandwich as well.

2	pounds Angus ground beef	2	large eggs, lightly beaten
¾	cup uncooked quick-cooking oats	1	teaspoon salt
1	medium onion, finely chopped	½	teaspoon black pepper
1	cup ketchup, divided	3	tablespoons dark brown sugar
¼	cup milk	2	teaspoons prepared mustard

Preheat the oven to 350 degrees. In a large bowl combine the ground beef, oats, onion, ½ cup of the ketchup, the milk, eggs, salt, and pepper. Shape into two 1-pound loaves. Place the loaves on an aluminum foil-lined pan. Bake for 40 minutes.

In a small bowl combine the remaining ½ cup of ketchup, the brown sugar and the mustard. Spoon over the meat loaf and bake for another 15 minutes, or until the meat thermometer reads 170-175 degrees. Slice and serve hot.

Makes 10 to 12 servings

FRED KING'S CAJUN MEATLOAF

3	pounds lean ground chuck		1	teaspoon dried oregano
1	pound ground pork		1	cup chopped olives with pimentos
1	pound ground veal		1	cup bread crumbs to bind mixture
3	large eggs			together
1	teaspoon Worcestershire sauce			
1	tablespoon salt		**Sauce**	
½	tablespoon Tabasco sauce		3	cups tomato sauce
2	cups chopped sweet onion		1	cup ketchup
½	cup chopped green bell pepper		1	cup dry white wine
1	cup chopped fresh parsley		1	teaspoon liquid smoke
2	tablespoons chopped garlic		1	tablespoon Worcestershire sauce

Preheat the oven to 350 degrees. In a large bowl combine the beef, pork, and veal mixing well. Add the eggs, Worcestershire, salt, Tabasco, onion, bell pepper, parsley, garlic, dried oregano, olives, and bread crumbs. Shape the mixture into 5 loaves. Place on an aluminum-foil-lined baking sheet. In a small bowl combine the tomato sauce, ketchup, dry white wine, liquid smoke, and Worcestershire sauce. Spoon over the meat loaf and bake for 40 minutes, or until the meat thermometer reads 170–175 degrees.

Makes 10 to 12 servings

BEEF ENCHILADAS

1	pound ground beef	¼	cup vegetable oil
1	large onion, chopped	12	corn tortillas
1½	tablespoons all-purpose flour	½	cup sliced ripe olives
1	tablespoon chili powder		Enchilada Sauce (recipe on next page)
1	teaspoon garlic powder		
¾	teaspoon salt	2	cups (8 ounces) shredded Monterey Jack cheese
¼	teaspoon ground cumin		
1	(16-ounce) can stewed tomatoes, undrained		

Preheat the oven to 350 degrees. Grease a 13 x 9-inch baking dish. In a large skillet, sauté the beef and onion until the meat is brown and crumbled. Drain the fat from the skillet and add the flour, chili powder, garlic powder, salt, and cumin. Cook for 1 minute, stirring constantly. Stir in the tomatoes, cooking just until thoroughly heated.

In a large skillet, heat the oil over medium-high heat. Fry the tortillas, one at a time, in the hot oil for 3 to 5 seconds on each side just to soften. Add more oil, if necessary. Drain on paper towels. Spoon 2 tablespoons of the meat mixture over the tortillas. Spread olive slices evenly over each tortilla. Roll up the tortilla and place seam-side down in the prepared baking dish. Pour enough Enchilada Sauce over the tortillas to cover. Bake for 15 minutes. Spread the cheese over top and bake for 5 to 10 minutes longer, or until the cheese is melted.

Makes 6 servings

CHICKEN ENCHILADAS

At Gabriel's we sell these in our frozen food section.

Enchilada Sauce
2   tablespoons olive oil
½   cup chopped onions
2   teaspoons chili powder
2   (8-ounce) cans tomato sauce
½   cup chicken broth
1   teaspoon cumin
     Salt and pepper, to taste

Enchiladas
1   (10¾-ounce) can cream of
     chicken soup
1   cup sour cream
3   to 4 cups cubed or shredded
     cooked chicken
1   (16-ounce) can refried beans
10   (6- to 8-inch) flour tortillas
3   cups shredded Cheddar cheese
¼   cup sliced green onions
¼   cup sliced green olives
¼   cup sliced black olives

Prepare the enchilada sauce. Heat the oil in a sauté pan over medium heat. Add the onions and sauté until transluscent. Add the chili powder, tomato sauce, chicken broth, cumin, and salt and pepper. Bring to a boil, stirring well.

For the enchiladas, preheat the oven to 350 degrees. Grease a 13 x 9-inch baking dish. In a large bowl combine the soup and sour cream, mixing well. Stir in the chicken pieces. Spread 2 tablespoons beans over each tortilla. Spread ⅓ cup of the chicken mixture down the center of each tortilla. Sprinkle with 1 tablespoon cheese. Roll up each tortilla and place seam-side down in the prepared baking dish.

Pour the Enchilada Sauce over the tortillas. Sprinkle with the green onions, green and black olives, and the remaining cheese. Bake for 35 minutes, or until bubbling.

Makes 6 to 8 servings

CHICKEN FAJITAS

This is my family's favorite fajita recipe. The chicken is grilled and adds great flavor. The only disadvantage you will have is not having my husband, Ed, there to do your grilling. He grills the best steak, chicken, and fish of anyone I know. I can't find salmon or a steak in any restaurant that's better than his. His grilling tips are on page 106 in this book. We served this at both of my daughters' graduation parties here at the house and numerous other casual gatherings.

1	cup bottled zesty Italian salad dressing	8	boneless, skinless chicken breast halves, cleaned and dried with paper towels
1	cup light soy sauce, divided	2	medium-size sweet or yellow onions
3	fresh limes, halved	16	flour tortillas
			Fresh cilantro, chopped

In a medium bowl combine the Italian dressing and $3/4$ cup of the soy sauce. Reserve $1/4$ cup of this mixture to sauté the onion slices. Add the juice of 1 fresh lime to the remaining marinade. Place the chicken breasts in a large dish or in a large zip-top bag. Pour the marinade over the breasts and refrigerate at least 1 hour or overnight.

Peel the onions and cut in half. Slice by hand into $1/4$-inch or thinner slices or use the slicing blade of a food processor to cut the onions. In a small skillet over medium-high heat, sauté the onions in the reserved marinade for 3 to 5 minutes. Set aside. Drain the chicken, reserving the marinade. Grill the chicken breasts over the hot fire about 5 minutes on each side, basting often with the reserved marinade. Squeeze two of the cut limes over the chicken and remove the chicken from the grill. Place the chicken on a cutting board and slice into $1/4$-inch-wide strips. Place on an aluminum-foil-wrapped plate to serve warm. Wrap the tortillas in paper towels and heat in the microwave oven for $1^1/2$ minutes or until hot. Transfer the tortillas to a serving basket, keeping covered and wrapped to serve them warm.

To serve, place the chicken strips on a warm tortilla and top with onion and chopped cilantro. Serve with salsa, guacamole, sour cream, and shredded cheese.

Makes 4 to 6 servings

SMOTHERED CHICKEN

Barbara Reilly, who lives in Marietta, shared this recipe with me. It was a dish her mother, Virginia McKinley, cooked frequently and is remembered by Barbara and her children with fond and loving memories of family gatherings.

1/3	cup all-purpose flour	1	(2.75-ounce) package dry chicken
1	teaspoon salt		noodle soup mix
1/8	teaspoon black pepper	1/2	cup water
4	boneless, skinless chicken breasts	1	medium onion, chopped
1/4	cup (1/2 stick) butter	1	(12-ounce) can evaporated milk

In a large plastic zip-top bag, mix the flour, salt, and pepper. Add the chicken and shake to coat the chicken with the flour mixture. In a 10-inch skillet melt the butter over medium heat. Add the chicken. Brown the chicken on both sides. Sprinkle the dry soup mix on and around the chicken pieces. Add the water and the chopped onion. Cook, covered, 30 to 35 minutes on low heat. Check the skillet periodically and add water if needed.

Remove the chicken from the skillet and place in a deep serving dish. Pour the evaporated milk into the skillet, stirring and cooking until your mixture is thick and hot but not boiling. Pour the sauce around the chicken, not over the top, to leave crisp noodles on the chicken pieces. Serve with rice pilaf.

Makes 4 servings

Roasted Chicken

We serve roasted chicken every day at Gabriel's as part of our "meat-and-two" menu.

1	(3- to 3½-pound) roasting chicken, cleaned, rinsed, and dried	½	lemon, studded with 2 cloves
	Mrs. Dash original salt-free seasoning blend	1	bay leaf
		2	to 3 sprigs fresh thyme
		2	teaspoons minced garlic

Preheat the oven to 350 degrees. Generously sprinkle the outside skin of the chicken with Mrs. Dash seasoning. Insert the lemon, bay leaf, thyme, and minced garlic into the cavity of the chicken. Place the chicken in a roasting pan breast side up. Roast the chicken for 1 hour and 15 minutes to 1 hour 30 minutes, or until the internal temperature in the thigh reaches 175 degrees or when the thigh is pricked and the juices run clear. Tent the chicken with aluminum foil for about 10 minutes. Remove from the oven. Carve, and serve hot.

Makes 4 to 6 servings

ED'S GRILLING TIPS

- Brush or spray a cold grill with oil to prevent sticking.
- Use zip-top bags to marinate meats or vegetables. Press out the air and seal. Set the bag in a large pan or baking dish, refrigerate, and turn occasionally.
- Glass baking dishes work well for marinating. Avoid aluminum, which will interact with acids in marinades.
- Trim excess fat from meat before grilling to avoid flare-ups. Cut fatty edges to keep meat from curling.
- Fill a spray bottle with water and a small amount of vinegar to spray the grill during flare-ups.
- Preheat gas grills at least 15 minutes. Light charcoal grills at least 45 minutes prior to grilling and let burn to hot embers coated with ash.
- Begin grilling when the temperature reaches 300 degrees Farenheit.
- Use your hand to determine approximate temperature. Hold your hand 3 inches above rack and count the seconds you can comfortably keep it in place: 5 seconds for low, 4 for medium, 3 for medium-high, and 2 for high.
- For small, delicate items, such as fish, shrimp or asparagus, use an oiled grill basket.
- Use long-handled tools and tongs—not forks—to turn meat to avoid piercing and releasing juices.
- To prevent scorching, brush the meat with prepared barbeque sauce only after the meat is cooked through.
- Some marinades may produce flare-ups. Be sure to keep a close watch on your food to prevent this or at least stop it when it occurs.

Dry-Rub Barbecued Chicken

This is another delicious recipe from the Dunaway family of Marietta. It requires a smoker.

6   to 8 small chicken leg quarters
1   tablespoon Shake and Bake powder
     (the original chicken blend)
1   tablespoon lemon pepper

Enough paprika to give the mixture
a light orange tint
Hickory chips

Wash and clean the chicken leg quarters. Trim off any excess fat or skin, but don't skin completely. In a large bowl or large zip-top bag, mix the Shake and Bake powder, lemon pepper, and paprika. Dredge the quarters in the dry mix. Place on the rack in an electric or charcoal smoker, using hickory chips for flavor. Do not put water in the smoker pan because the chicken needs to dry a little. (This recipe can be done with a grill, but chicken should be cooked with low indirect heat, putting the hickory chips in a pan for the smoke flavor.) Smoke for 1 to 1½ hours, or until the legs move easily.

Makes 4 to 6 servings

NOTE: Breast quarters do not work as well with this method because the thin part of the wing burns before the thicker breast cooks.

CHICKEN PENNE PASTA WITH TOMATO CREAM SAUCE

¼ cup olive oil plus 1 tablespoon
   olive oil
1 tablespoon chopped garlic
1 tablespoon chopped fresh rosemary
   Salt and pepper, to taste
4 to 6 chicken breasts, skin removed
1 (28-ounce) can Italian tomatoes
1 tablespoon butter

1 small onion, chopped
1 cup whipping cream
¼ cup vodka
¼ teaspoon dried crushed red pepper
1 pound penne pasta
   Freshly grated Parmesan cheese
   Minced fresh chives

In a 13 x 9-inch baking dish, mix ¼ cup of the olive oil, the garlic, and the rosemary. Salt and pepper the chicken breasts, and place in the marinade, turning to coat. Cover the dish and refrigerate 4 hours or overnight, turning occasionally.

Drain the tomatoes, remove the seeds, and chop into bite-size pieces. In a heavy large saucepan, melt the butter with the remaining tablespoon of oil over medium heat. Add the onion, sautéing 6 to 8 minutes or until translucent. Add the tomatoes. Cook the vegetables, stirring frequently, for about 25 minutes, or until almost no liquid remains in the pan. Add the cream, vodka, and red pepper. Boil about 2 minutes, or until thickened. Season the mixture with salt and pepper as needed. (The sauce can be prepared one day ahead if covered and refrigerated.) Remove the breasts from the marinade, and place on a hot barbecue grill. Cook the chicken over medium-high heat for 10 to 12 minutes, turning occasionally until thoroughly cooked. Cool the chicken, and cut into bite-size pieces. Set aside.

In a large pot of boiling salted water, cook the penne pasta, stirring occasionally, until just tender but still firm to the bite. Drain well, and place in a large bowl. Add the chopped chicken to the sauce and reheat to a simmer. Pour the sauce and chicken over the pasta, and toss well. Sprinkle with Parmesan cheese and chives before serving.

Makes 8 servings

Low-Fat Garlic Lime Chicken

This is a really tasty low-fat way to cook chicken. It is good served warm with a side of vegetables, on a sandwich with mozzarella cheese, on a sandwich with fresh tomato slices and Bibb lettuce, or served cold on a Caesar salad.

½	cup low-sodium soy sauce	4	boneless, skinless chicken breast halves
¼	cup fresh lime juice		
1	tablespoon Worcestershire sauce	½	teaspoon coarsely ground black pepper
2	garlic cloves, minced		Olive oil-flavored cooking spray
½	teaspoon dry mustard		

In a small bowl whisk together the soy sauce, lime juice, Worcestershire, garlic, and dry mustard. Place the chicken in a zip-top bag, and pour the marinade over the breasts. Refrigerate 30 minutes. Drain the chicken, and sprinkle with black pepper. Grill the chicken breasts over medium heat 5 to 6 minutes on each side. (The chicken can also be prepared by spraying a nonstick skillet with olive oil-flavored cooking spray. Warm the oil over medium heat. Add the chicken, and cook about 6 minutes on each side or until a fork inserted into the chicken produces juice that runs clear and chicken is easily pierced.)

Makes 4 servings

SKILLET FRIED CHICKEN

From Executive Chef Thomas McEachern of Rays on the River, Atlanta

1/4	cup plus 1 teaspoon Kosher salt, divided	1/2	cup country ham pieces
1	quart (4 cups) water	1	cup all-purpose flour
1	(3-pound) chicken, cut into 8 pieces	2	tablespoons cornstarch
1	quart (4 cups) buttermilk	1/2	teaspoon onion powder
1	pound lard	1/2	teaspoon garlic powder
1/2	cup (1 stick) unsalted butter	1/2	teaspoon freshly ground black pepper

Combine the 1/4 cup salt and water in a large bowl. Add the chicken pieces. Refrigerate the chicken in the brine for 8 to 12 hours.

To prepare the chicken for frying, drain the brine from the chicken. Place the chicken in a large bowl, and cover the chicken with the buttermilk. Refrigerate 8 to 12 hours.

In a large heavy skillet, melt the lard and the butter. Add the country ham and cook over low heat for 30 minutes, or until the ham is browned. Do not allow the oil to brown. Skim to remove the foam (milk solids) from the butter. Drain the chicken from the buttermilk.

In a small bowl blend the flour, cornstarch, onion powder, garlic powder, the remaining teaspoon of salt, and the pepper. Dredge the chicken pieces thoroughly in the flour mixture. Pat each piece well to remove all excess flour. Just before frying, increase the temperature to medium-high (approximately 335 degrees). Place the chicken pieces skin-side down into the heated fat. Do not overcrowd the pan. Fry in batches, if necessary. Cook for 8 to 10 minutes on each side until the chicken is golden brown and cooked through. Drain thoroughly on a wire rack or paper towels.

Makes 6 servings

NOTE: Brining injects flavors and moisture into meats and poultry. It will give you the most moist poultry you have ever eaten.

SMOKED TURKEY

This is my husband's specialty during the holidays. It is extremely moist and flavorful and so easy.

1   (10- to 15-pound) turkey, thawed and cleaned, skin on
1   (9-ounce) jar yellow mustard

Ed uses a Cooking Cajun Smoker, but any smoker with a good-size water pan will work. The top needs to be tall enough to fit over the turkey, and the grill rack needs to be large enough to accommodate the turkey size. Soak 3 to 4 fistfuls of hardwood chunks in water for at least 1 hour. Build a fire in the bottom of the smoker with 10 pounds of charcoal and put the hardwood directly on the hot coals. Fill the water pan, and place it in the smoker. Dry any moisture off the skin of the turkey with paper towels. Using your hands, smear a heavy coat of mustard all over the turkey.

Place the turkey on the grill rack and cover, letting the turkey smoke at least 8 hours. (Ed usually puts the turkey on to smoke just before he goes to bed and it's ready the next morning.) Remove the turkey from the grill and serve immediately, or wrap it in aluminum foil to hold until serving time. Refrigerate if holding longer than 2 hours.

Makes 8 to 10 servings

CHERRY PORK LOIN

A simple but tasty entrée from my friend Saundra Fleming

3	pounds boneless pork loin	1/4	cup slivered almonds
	Salt and pepper, to taste	1/4	teaspoon salt
1	(12-ounce) jar whole cherry preserves	1/4	teaspoon ground nutmeg
2	teaspoons light corn syrup	1/4	teaspoon ground cinnamon
1/4	cup red wine vinegar		

Preheat the oven to 350 degrees. Rub the pork roast with salt and pepper. Roast, uncovered, 2 1/2 hours, or until the meat thermometer reaches 185 degrees.

In a small saucepan heat the preserves, corn syrup, vinegar, almonds, salt, nutmeg, and cinnamon to boiling. Reduce the heat to simmer and cook 2 minutes. Spoon the glaze over the roast and return to the oven for 15 minutes.

Makes 6 to 8 servings

GEORGE BROWN'S PORK TENDERLOIN WITH BARBECUE SAUCE

My friend Maria Geros shared this recipe from her dad, the late George Brown of Marietta. It is one of our favorite dishes to serve when we entertain.

¾ cup white vinegar	1 tablespoon Worcestershire sauce
¼ cup vegetable oil	1 medium onion, chopped
¼ cup water plus 2 tablespoons	1½ cups firmly packed dark brown sugar
1 tablespoon dry mustard	2½ to 3 pounds pork tenderloins,
3 cloves garlic, minced	cleaned of fat and silver skin
½ to 1 teaspoon salt	1 cup ketchup

Preheat a charcoal or gas grill to medium. In a 2-quart saucepan, mix the vinegar, oil, water, dry mustard, garlic, salt, Worcestershire, onion, and brown sugar. Bring to a boil, simmering until the onion is tender. Cook the tenderloins on the grill, basting generously with the sauce. Turn the pork, baste again, and cook to medium rare, 140 degrees. Whisk the ketchup into the basting sauce and bring back to a boil. Baste the loins again, cooking to about 160 degrees. The juices should run clear. Cut the pork into ½-inch medallions, and serve hot with the remaining warmed sauce.

Makes 8 servings

BOURBON-MARINATED AND LIGHTLY SMOKED PORK TENDERLOIN

From Executive Chef Thomas McEachern of Rays on the River, Atlanta

2	cups teriyaki		4	(8-ounce) portions pork tenderloin
1½	cups firmly packed dark brown sugar		3	tablespoons Dijon mustard
2	cups bourbon		3	tablespoons olive oil
1	sprig rosemary, leaves removed from the stem			

Preheat the oven to 400 degrees. In a medium bowl combine the teriyaki, brown sugar, bourbon, and rosemary leaves. Add the tenderloin to marinate for 10 minutes. Save the marinade. Place the pork in a stove-top smoker and lightly smoke for 4 minutes. After smoking, brush the pork with the Dijon mustard.

In a large ovenproof skillet, heat the olive oil, and sear the pork in the oil on all sides at a high heat until the meat is a golden brown. Pour the marinade over the pork and into the skillet, and place the pan in the oven. Braise for approximately 10 minutes, or until a meat thermometer stuck into the central part of the pork reads 160 degrees. Remove the pan from the oven, and let the pork rest for 5 minutes before slicing. Save the liquid in the pan. Slice the pork and use the pan drippings as the sauce.

Makes 4 servings

BARBEQUED PORK RIBS

2 racks baby back pork ribs
   (about 5 pounds total)
1 (28- to 40-ounce) bottle barbeque
   sauce
1 teaspoon cayenne pepper
1 teaspoon black pepper

2 teaspoons chili powder
1 teaspoon salt
2 teaspoons liquid smoke
1/4 cup ketchup
1/2 cup vinegar

Preheat the grill on high, and preheat the oven to 350 degrees. Rinse the ribs and pat them dry. On a hot grill, sear the ribs 5 minutes on each side. In a medium bowl, whisk together the barbeque sauce and the remaining ingredients, mixing well. Heavily brush both sides of the ribs with sauce, and place them in a roasting pan. Pour additional sauce over the top of the ribs to make sure they remain moist. Cover the pan with foil, and bake in the oven for about 3 hours. Uncover the ribs the last 15 to 20 minutes of roasting time.

In a saucepan heat the remaining barbeque sauce to almost simmering, being careful not to burn or scorch it. Remove the ribs from the roasting pan, and brush again generously with the barbeque sauce before serving.

Makes 6 servings

RACK OF LAMB WITH GARLIC AND MINT

My friend Trish Elliott contributed this recipe. It is one of the best I've ever eaten.

2   or 3 whole garlic bulbs
1/2   cup extra virgin olive oil, divided
1 1/2   cups rock salt
2   cups fresh mint leaves
8   cloves garlic, chopped

2   tablespoons Kosher salt
2   teaspoons freshly ground pepper
3   (2- to 2 1/2-pound, 8-rib) lamb rib
    roasts, trimmed

Preheat the oven to 425 degrees. Remove most of the skin from the garlic bulbs and rub down with 1/8 to 1/4 cup of the olive oil. Place them in a small roasting pan, and surround them with the rock salt. Roast for 35 to 45 minutes. (The rock salt will not make them salty but covers the bottom of the pan. No need to use the salt if you have a crock that is just for roasting garlic.) Set the garlic aside.

Preheat the oven to 400 degrees. In a food processor, blend the remaining olive oil, the mint leaves, chopped garlic, Kosher salt and ground pepper until smooth. Evenly spread the mixture over the roasts. On a rack in a large pan, place the lamb roasts fat side up, and roast for 10 minutes. Reduce the oven temperature to 375 degrees, and roast for 30 minutes, or until a meat thermometer placed in the center of the roasts reads 145 degrees.

Remove the lamb from the oven, cover loosely with aluminum foil, and let stand until the thermometers reads 150 degrees, which is medium rare. (Lamb is medium at 160 degrees. If you like your lamb medium, roast until thermometer reads 155 degrees and let stand to 160 degrees.) Insert a sharp knife between the ribs and slice into individual chops. Garnish with the whole bulbs of garlic and extra mint leaves to serve.

Makes 10 to 12 servings

ROAST LEG OF LAMB WITH GOAT CHEESE, HERBS, AND BREAD CRUMB CRUST

Evans Nichols is a first-generation Greek-American. He cooks the best lamb of anyone I know. A dinner invitation from Evans and his wife, Dee, means the food is going to be great.

4	tablespoons plus 1 teaspoon olive oil, divided	4	to 6 ounces goat cheese, softened
3	tablespoons fresh rosemary	3	to 4 pounds boneless half leg of lamb, untied
3	garlic cloves, peeled		Salt and fresh ground black pepper, to taste
2	teaspoons fresh thyme		Additional olive oil
1/4	cup fresh parsley		
1/4	cup Parmesan cheese	2	tablespoons Dijon mustard
1	cup fresh bread crumbs		

Preheat the oven to 375 degrees. In a food processor using a steel blade, combine the 1 teaspoon of olive oil, the rosemary, garlic, thyme, and parsley. Mince the mixture. Remove and reserve 1 1/2 tablespoons of the mixture in a small bowl. Scrape the remaining mixture into a medium bowl, and stir in Parmesan cheese, bread crumbs, and 1 tablespoon of the olive oil. Set aside. Combine the reserved 1 1/2 tablespoons of the garlic mixture with the goat cheese and set aside.

Lay the lamb with the rough surface up and pound to a 3/4-inch thickness. Rub with 1 tablespoon of the olive oil, and season with salt and pepper. Spread the goat cheese mixture on the lamb. Roll the lamb into a tight cylinder, and tie with butcher's twine. In a hot, heavy, large skillet, heat the remaining 2 tablespoons of olive oil. Add the lamb, and sear on all sides and each end.

Transfer the seared lamb to a roasting rack on a rimmed baking sheet and roast with the rack on the lower to middle position of the oven for 30 minutes, or until the internal temperature is 120 degrees in the thickest part of the meat.

Transfer the lamb to a cutting board, and carefully remove and discard the twine. Brush the lamb entirely with olive oil, and apply a thin layer of Dijon mustard. Carefully press the herb bread crumb mixture to form an even crust coating the lamb.

Return the lamb to the rack for an additional 15 to 25 minutes, or until the internal temperature is 130 to 135 degrees for medium-rare lamb or 160 degrees for medium. Transfer the meat to a cutting board, and tent with aluminum foil for 10 to 15 minutes. Cut into 1/2-inch slices and serve.

Makes 6 to 8 servings

CRAB CAKES WITH JALAPEÑO LIME MAPLE SYRUP SAUCE

When we serve crab cakes at Gabriel's, this is the recipe we use—originally from Connie Kirk and Diane Cooper.

1	cup fresh lime juice	4	tablespoons Dijon mustard
4	jalapeño peppers, seeded and diced	3	dashes Tabasco sauce
2	tablespoons maple syrup		Salt and pepper, to taste
4	cloves garlic, finely chopped	2	large eggs
½	cup mayonnaise (not light)		Panko bread crumbs
16	ounces crab (lump tastes best or use 8 ounces lump and 8 ounces Special* crabmeat), drained		Peanut oil for frying

In a medium bowl mix the lime juice, jalapeños, maple syrup, and garlic. Refrigerate overnight. Strain the sauce before using. In a medium bowl mix the mayonnaise, crabmeat, mustard, Tabasco, salt, pepper, and eggs. Form the mixture into five cakes if using for an entrée or scoop large, rounded tablespoons if using for an appetizer. Pack the crabmeat firmly so the cakes hold their shape. Place the cakes on a cookie sheet lined with parchment. Chill for 3 hours. When ready to cook, coat the cakes with the bread crumbs. Fry in small amount of peanut oil for 2 minutes on each side. Drain on paper towels. Serve with the jalapeño sauce.

Makes 5 (4.5-ounce) servings

NOTE: Cakes may be reheated in a 350-degree oven for 6 minutes.

* "Special" crabmeat is part of the name on the crab container; this meat is merely pieces of lump crabmeat that broke up when being picked or packed.

Tom's Crab Cakes

From Executive Chef Thomas McEachern of Rays on the River, Atlanta

1¼	cups mayonnaise	2	red bell peppers, roasted, peeled, seeded, and chopped
1	large egg		
2	large egg yolks	6	scallions, white part only, minced
½	ounce lemon juice	⅛	cup parsley, chopped
⅛	teaspoon celery seed	1	jalapeño pepper, minced and seeded
½	teaspoon garlic powder		
¼	teaspoon dry mustard	16	ounces Special crabmeat
1¼	teaspoon salt	1¼	cups crumbled Ritz crackers
¼	teaspoon whole black pepper, ground	16	ounces jumbo lump crabmeat
		1	cup vegetable oil

Combine the mayonnaise, egg, egg yolks, lemon juice, celery seed, garlic powder, dry mustard, salt, black pepper, red bell peppers, scallions, parsley, and jalapeño pepper. Fold in the Special crabmeat and cracker crumbs. Carefully fold in the jumbo lump crabmeat. Using your hands, mold the crab into ten cakes about ½ inch thick. Place them on a cookie sheet or plate and cover with plastic wrap. Refrigerate for 1 hour before cooking. In a large nonstick skillet, heat the oil over medium high heat. Fill the bottom of the skillet with crab cakes, leaving about ½ inch between cakes. Cook each crab cake about 5 minutes on each side, turning only once until cakes are golden brown and crispy on each side. Serve hot or reheat in a 200-degree oven before serving. Serve with Spicy Remoulade Sauce (recipe on the next page) or lemon butter sauce.

Make 5 servings

Spicy Remoulade Sauce

Judy Watts, a gracious and talented hostess, supplied this recipe.

2	tomatoes, quartered	2	tablespoons capers plus juice
2	large jalapeño pepper, washed, stem removed, and quartered	1	quart (4 cups) mayonnaise
½	small onion	6	cornichons
			Juice of ½ lemon

Place all the tomatoes, jalapeños, onion, capers, mayonnaise, cornichons, and lemon juice in the container of a food processor. Whip until well blended. This sauce is good with any seafood and cold meats. This sauce will keep for 30 days in the refrigerator.

Makes 1½ quarts (8 cups)

Tom's Crab Cakes (page 122)

Sautéed Shrimp over White Cheddar Grits

From Executive Chef Thomas McEachern of Rays on the River, Atlanta

1/2	cup plus 1 tablespoon olive oil, divided		2	tablespoons finely minced garlic
3	cups sliced yellow onion			Chili flakes, as desired
3	to 4 red bell peppers		1/2	cup cream sherry
2 1/2	pounds large or extra large shrimp		1/2	cup (1 stick) unsalted butter
	Salt and pepper, to taste			White Cheddar Grits
				Chopped flat-leaf parsley, for garnish

In a large skillet heat 1/4 cup of the olive oil over medium heat. Add the onions, and reduce the heat to low. Cook for about 20 minutes, or until the onions are soft and have a little color, stirring occasionally. Turn the heat lower if the onions start to become more than slightly colored. Remove from the heat and set aside.

Preheat the oven to 400 degrees. Rub the peppers with about 1 tablespoon of the olive oil, and place them in a roasting pan. Roast 30 to 40 minutes or until charred on all sides, turning occasionally. Remove the peppers from the oven, and place them in a bowl covered with plastic. Steam for 5 to 10 minutes. Peel the skin from the peppers and discard. Remove the core and seeds, and slice into 2 cups of strips. Set aside.

In a very large skillet heat the remaining 5 tablespoons of olive oil. Sauté the shrimp over high heat for approximately 1 minute. (Add more olive oil if necessary). Add the garlic and chili flakes. Continue to sauté over high heat for approximately 2 minutes. Add the caramelized onion, the roasted red pepper, and the cream sherry. Reduce the mixture over high heat for approximately 2 minutes. Add the butter, stirring constantly until melted. Remove the skillet from the heat.

Serve the shrimp immediately over White Cheddar Grits, and garnish with the chopped parsley.

Makes 8 servings

White Cheddar Grits

2   cups half-and-half
1   cup stone-ground grits
2   cups chicken broth plus an extra ¼
    cup, if needed

¼   pound sharp white Cheddar cheese,
    grated
    Salt and pepper, to taste

In a 2- to 3-quart heavy and well-insulated saucepan, bring the half-and-half to a boil. Add the grits and reduce the heat. Simmer until thick, stirring constantly. Add the 2 cups chicken broth ¼ cup at a time until absorbed. Add the cheese, stirring constantly. Add salt and pepper. (Add more broth if necessary.)

Makes 8 servings

THE BEST SALMON YOU'LL EVER EAT

I have had dinner once a month for thirty years with the same ten to twelve women, my Birthday Club. Once a year it is my time to hostess the club. This recipe from our friend Carl Reinhard is their request every year. My husband, Ed, has the magic touch on the grill. Carl tells us this recipe is good with other fish as well. At Gabriel's we roast the salmon using this sauce to make our salmon salad and/or a fillet sandwich. It's almost as good roasted in the oven as it is on the grill.

½	pound butter	1	garlic clove, chopped
4	tablespoons soy sauce	2½	to 3 pounds of a fresh side of salmon,
2	tablespoons prepared mustard		skin and bones removed, cut into
3	tablespoons Worcestershire sauce		2 pieces
¼	cup ketchup		

In a small saucepan whisk together the butter, soy sauce, mustard, Worcestershire, ketchup, and garlic. Cook over medium heat until nearly boiling and well blended. Set aside half of the sauce to serve with the cooked salmon.

Heat a charcoal or gas grill to medium to medium high. Baste one side of the salmon, and place on the grill sauce side down, grilling for 5 to 6 minutes. Baste the top, and turn the salmon over. Repeat basting on the top side, and cook about 5 minutes, depending on the thickness of the fish. Remove the fish from the grill to a warm plate. If not serving immediately, or if you're not sure you have the doneness desired, put the salmon on a baking sheet, wrap with foil, and place in a preheated, 350-degree oven. Serve with the extra sauce.

Makes 6 servings

NOTE: To roast, baste both sides of the salmon and place on an aluminum foil-lined pan. Roast in a 350-degree convection oven for 20 to 30 minutes or until the salmon flakes easily. If using a conventional oven, roast for 30 to 40 minutes at 350 degrees.

SHRIMP SINATRA BUBBALINI

Dennis and Flo Rowley serve this dish in Bubbalini's, their Italian restaurant that's in the same shopping center as Gabriel's Desserts. The Rowleys are great friends as well as neighbors, and their food is delicious.

3	ounces olive oil	¼	cup white wine
2	tablespoons chopped garlic	10	ounces heavy cream
	Salt, to taste	12	strips sun-dried tomatoes
1	teaspoon white pepper	2	tablespoons dried oregano
8	colossal shrimp, peeled and deveined	4	cups cooked linguine, drained

In a large saucepan heat the olive oil over medium heat. When hot, add the garlic. Sprinkle salt and white pepper on each shrimp. Add the shrimp to the saucepan, and sauté for 1 minute. Turn the shrimp, and sauté on the opposite side for 1 minute. Add the white wine, heavy cream, sun-dried tomatoes, oregano, salt, and white pepper as needed. Remove the shrimp from the pan while the cream reduces to avoid overcooking them. When the sauce has thickened, add the shrimp back into the sauté pan. Add the cooked linguine, coating it with the sauce. Serve in individual pasta bowls, positioning the shrimp on the top.

Makes 2 servings

GROUPER PEPPERONCINI DIJON

Dennis and Flo Rowley of Bubbalini's Restaurant in Marietta share another one of their recipes. The Rowleys are true restaurateurs . . . hard working, persevering, and appreciative of every one of their customers.

2	(8- to 10-ounce) grouper fillets			Pinch of salt
	All-purpose flour			Pinch of white pepper
	Olive oil		10	ounces heavy cream
6	pepperoncini, sliced into rings		2	tablespoon butter
4	tablespoons Dijon mustard		4	cups cooked penne pasta
½	cup white wine			

Preheat the oven to 375 degrees. Dredge the grouper in flour and set aside.

In a 10-inch ovenproof sauté pan, heat just enough olive oil on medium-high heat to sear the grouper. Add the fillets, searing on both sides until golden. Put the sauté pan into the oven to finish cooking the grouper for about 10 minutes. Check often so as not to overcook, especially if the fillets are thin.

While the grouper is cooking, heat another sauté pan over medium heat. Add the pepperoncini and mustard. When heated, whisk in the white wine, salt, and white pepper. After the wine and mustard are combined, add the heavy cream and butter. Reduce to thicken. Remove the grouper from the oven, and place on two dinner plates. Pour half the sauce on the fillets. Add the penne pasta to the remaining sauce in the pan, mixing well to coat the pasta with the sauce. Place the pasta on the plate next to the grouper.

Makes 2 servings

TIP: Searing is the browning or caramelizing of food over high heat. A small amount of fat is used. Searing brings out the flavor and creates a fond on the bottom of the pan that is used for making sauces.

SOUTHERN HOSPITALITY

*M*uch practiced in the South and talked about by others is the region's hospitality. Hopefully, those who visit experience it. I can't imagine it not being a part of my life. I have traveled a little, not extensively, but remember once in a Western coastal state being told by a friend not to smile at everyone I passed. It just didn't feel normal not to look people in the eye and smile.

Hospitality didn't begin with Southerners. We might like to try, but we can't claim exclusive rights. I have read of its practice as far back as Biblical times. When a stranger or visitor arrived, there was water to drink, sometimes even a foot washing, and a meal was prepared. We Southerners follow those traditions closely, usually omitting the foot washing, as most of us are no longer traveling by foot on dusty roads. Certainly drinks and food are offered on most any occasion. Just give us a reason.

All the major events of life are celebrated with drinks and food. Births, weddings, serious illnesses, funerals, promotions, graduations, and house moves give us the opportunity to congregate, commiserate, or celebrate with fellowship and food. I am a great lover of good food, of course, but think many of us use those occasions to "visit" and "catch up" with friends and neighbors. Good food and drink keeps them staying a while longer.

Southerners are especially famous for our food and gatherings after a funeral. Friends usually bring dishes upon dishes of their best recipe that can be served to the family and friends of the deceased. Gathering at the deceased's house or that of a close relative almost serves as a family reunion. Talk and laughter about the loved one occurs, with both good and bad times discussed. Then we move on and find out who's married, divorced, had babies, or become grandparents. Often politics are even discussed.

Recently, one of my close friend's mother died. At the funeral all family members and friends were invited by the house to enjoy a meal and visit with the family. In a short span of two days, a reception for fifty to sixty people had been organized. The table was laden with meats, casseroles, vegetables, and desserts. By the time the visitors left, a crew of folks in the kitchen had put away the food, washed the dishes, and returned the house to as normal a state as possible. Had I planned to have 50 people to my house for dinner, I would have planned for a month, but with phone calls and covered dishes this was taken care of in two days.

The hardest part for the host family member is returning all the dishes that come in. Most of the time we put a little sticker with our name on the dish on the bottom so that it can be returned, but invariably I have ended up with one unclaimed bowl.

I think the next time I take a covered dish, I'll prepare it in one of those unclaimed dishes. Eventually the real owner will see it at a gathering and mention that she "lost" a dish just like that, and I can offer it right back to her. The rule of thumb in sending these dishes is not to send your worst-looking dish, but don't send your best one either.

Southern hospitality extends beyond friends and family. We truly welcome others who come South for a visit or to live. Why are we so interested in others? Inquiring about others and events in their lives or where they come from, gives me facts about them—facts that give me a point of reference so that I can remember them, rather than a face without any information.

Oftentimes when Southerners hear of misfortune in a person's life, we give them a blessing: "Bless your heart." That tells a person that we praise their courage and fortitude and wish better for them. From a personal standpoint,

Raspberry Grits (page 38)

it calls us to wonder if we too could hold up under those same circumstances and secretly pray that it never happens to us.

"Bless your heart" can also mean "thank you." It is said if someone compliments you on the way you look or a job you did, you are flattered, but don't know how to accept and "bless your heart" just comes right out. It can also be used to say thank you for a gift: "Bless your heart, how did you know I wanted that?" We receive good things and reciprocate with a blessing. Not a bad way to live and think. Hopefully, we'll remember to share all these blessings with those who truly need them, not just part of a polite conversation.

Perhaps our reasonably mild weather and changing seasons add to our willingness to share our part of the planet. There are days on end of beautiful sunshine, even when temperatures are low. We have fierce summer thunderstorms that command respect for nature and put on a first-class light show. We have early spring flowers and then more flowers that stay in bloom until a frost. Breathtaking fall colors amaze me year after year. We have mountains, valleys, and beaches that are within a few hours drive of each other. With all this beauty, how can we not be proud and willing to share?

For some reason, Southerners in general seem happy to meet and greet strangers—and each other—and it just doesn't seem to be as much fun without food and drink. I hope it's a tradition we keep forever.

SIDE DISHES

Southerners Love Their Veggies

Nana's Deluxe Rice Dish

As my children were growing up many Christmas Eves were spent at my good friend Carole Simpson's house. We all attended the candlelight service at our church and then packed her house with children, adults, gifts, and lots of good food. Both of our mothers were widows and these evenings with them and family hold a very special place in my memory. Carole's mother, Nana, always brought this dish. It is simple and delicious.

1½ cups rice	1 (4-ounce) package sliced almonds,
1¼ cups (2½ sticks) butter	skins on, divided
3 cups beef broth, heated	Fresh or dried parsley, to taste

Grease a 13 x 9-inch baking dish. Wash the rice in a colander, draining well. In a medium skillet melt the butter over medium heat. Add the rice and sauté until browned. Remove from the heat, stir in half the almonds, and spread the rice mixture into the prepared baking dish. Pour the hot beef broth over the rice and let soak 6 to 8 hours.

When ready to serve preheat the oven to 425 degrees. Add the remaining almonds over the top and sprinkle with parsley. Bake for 10 to 20 minutes, or until the liquid is absorbed but not dry. Serve hot.

Makes 8 servings

Parmesan Rice Bake

1¾ cups water
1 cup Basmati rice
⅓ cup vegetable oil, divided
1 large egg, beaten
½ cup chopped fresh parsley
4 ounces shredded sharp Cheddar
  cheese

1 medium onion, chopped
1 teaspoon salt
1 (10¾-ounce) can cream of
  celery soup
1½ cups grated Parmesan cheese
1½ cups bread crumbs
¼ cup (½ stick) butter, sliced

Coat a 2-quart baking dish with nonstick cooking spray. In a medium saucepan bring the water and 2 tablespoons of the vegetable oil to a boil over high heat. Add the rice, reduce the temperature to low, cover, and simmer for 20 minutes.

Preheat the oven to 350 degrees. In a medium bowl combine the egg, the remaining oil, parsley, Cheddar cheese, onion, salt, and celery soup. Add the cooked rice. Spread the rice in the prepared casserole dish, and sprinkle with the Parmesan cheese. Spread the bread crumbs over the cheese and dot with the butter slices. Bake for 30 minutes

Makes 6 to 8 servings

GOURMET RICE WITH MUSHROOMS AND PECANS

½   cup (1 stick) butter
1   cup long-grain wild rice, without
     seasoning
½   cup chopped pecans
1   small onion, chopped

1   (5-ounce) jar mushrooms, drained
2   cups water
4   chicken bouillon cubes or the
     equivalent in granules

Preheat the oven to 325 degrees. Coat a 13 x 9-inch baking dish with nonstick cooking spray. In a large skillet, melt the stick of butter over medium heat, without browning. Add the rice, pecans, onion, and mushrooms to the skillet. Sauté the mixture for 5 to 7 minutes. Place the rice in the prepared baking dish. Heat the water and add the chicken bouillon, stirring to dissolve. Pour over the rice, and bake the casserole 1 hour.

Makes 8 servings

BRAISED GREENS

From Executive Chef Thomas McEachern of Rays on the River, Atlanta

½	pound Applewood-smoked bacon, julienned	1	tablespoon black pepper
½	pound onions, diced	1	quart (4 cups) chicken broth
1	cup red wine vinegar	1½	pounds collards, turnip greens, or mustard greens, chopped
⅓	cup sugar	1	tablespoon salt

Use a large skillet to sauté the bacon. Add the onion, sautéing until translucent. Deglaze the pan with the red wine vinegar. Add the sugar and the black pepper. Continue to cook until the mixture reduces to a syrup. Add the chicken broth, bring to a boil, and then add the mix of greens and the salt. Reduce the temperature to a simmer, and cook for approximately 20 minutes.

Makes 2 quarts (8 cups)

COLLARDS OR TURNIP GREENS

*Cynthia Robinson is our deli manager and turns out fine Southern vegetables daily at Gabriel's.
The seasoning of the vegetables is truly her talent. She has been cooking since her early teens, and our
customers benefit from her experience on a daily basis. Her seasonings are the traditional Southern ones,
but she adds her own personal touches here and there that always seem to enhance the flavor of the dish.
We serve fresh turnips, collards or cooked cabbage every day at the restaurant. I never fail to include them
on my lunch plate.*

1	gallon (16 cups) water	7	tablespoons chicken base
1	green bell pepper, cut in half and seeded	7	tablespoons bacon fat
½	large onion, cut in half	½	teaspoon red pepper flakes
⅓	cup sugar	4	pounds prewashed and chopped collards or turnip greens

In a large stockpot combine the water, bell pepper, onion, sugar, chicken base,
bacon fat, and red pepper flakes. Cover and bring to a boil. Reduce the heat and
simmer, uncovered, 30 minutes. Add the greens, and continue to simmer,
uncovered, for 2 hours. The turnips or collards will wilt down and be covered by
the water.

Makes 16 to 20 servings

NOTE: In the past when I cleaned and chopped my own collards and turnips,
instead of buying them prechopped, I would remove practically all of the stems,
getting rid of a lot of the fiber. Now at Gabriel's, we leave a fair amount of the
stems for the fiber.

BLACK-EYED PEAS

A Southern favorite, as well as a staple at Gabriel's. Lots of southerners want diced raw onions with their peas and hot cornbread muffins.

6   cups water
1   tablespoon chicken base
½   teaspoon sugar
½   onion, chopped

½   green bell pepper, chopped
½   teaspoon Kosher salt
20   ounces of fresh or frozen black-eyed peas

In a 3- to 4-quart saucepan, bring the water, chicken base, sugar, onion, bell pepper, and salt to a boil. Reduce the heat and simmer over low heat for about 20 to 30 minutes. Add the black-eyed peas and continue to simmer for 1 hour. Add more water as needed to "almost" keep the peas covered.

Makes 12 to 14 servings

SPINACH CASSEROLE

This casserole is for spinach lovers since there are not a lot of other ingredients in it. The original recipe was given to me by a former employee, Michael Whatley. Michael loves to cook, and it just seems to come naturally to him. Spinach Casserole is now a favorite at Gabriel's.

2	pounds frozen spinach	¼	cup chicken base
¼	cup (½ stick) unsalted butter	1½	cups heavy cream
2	tablespoons minced garlic	2	cups grated Parmesan cheese, divided

Preheat the oven to 350 degrees. Grease a medium casserole dish. Put the frozen spinach in a colander, and as it thaws, press out as much water as possible. In a medium skillet, melt the butter over medium heat, and sauté the garlic until fragrant. Add the chicken base and the thawed spinach, cooking long enough to warm the spinach. Gradually add the cream and 1 cup of the cheese. Put the spinach mixture into the prepared dish. Bake for 15 minutes. Sprinkle the remaining 1 cup Parmesean cheese on top and return to the oven for 15 more minutes.

Makes 6 to 8 servings

SQUASH CASSEROLE

One of Gabriel's most requested vegetables, this squash casserole has no creamed soup filler . . . just squash, onions, and cheese.

2	pounds yellow squash, washed and sliced	2	cups saltines or Ritz cracker crumbs, divided
1	onion, chopped	1	cup Cheddar cheese, grated
3	tablespoons parsley flakes Salt and pepper, to taste	¼	cup milk

Roast the squash and onion in the oven, or boil in a large saucepan, covered with water, until the vegetables are tender. Drain well. Preheat the oven to 350 degrees. Coat a 13 x 9-inch baking pan with nonstick cooking spray. In a medium bowl, mix the squash and onion, parsley flakes, salt and pepper, and 1 cup of the cracker crumbs. Place the mixture in the prepared pan. Combine the remaining 1 cup cracker crumbs and the Cheddar cheese. Spread over the top of the casserole. Bake for 25 minutes.

Makes 8 servings

TIP: If you have time, roasting vegetables in the oven at 350 degrees until tender adds a little extra flavor. Because of the quantity that we prepare at Gabriel's, we boil in just enough water to cover until tender.

ZUCCHINI CASSEROLE

One of Gabriel's recipes where the Rotel tomatoes with diced chile peppers add a little "kick."

5	medium zucchini, cut into ¼-inch pieces	¼	teaspoon oregano
¼	cup olive oil	¼	teaspoon basil
1	garlic clove, minced	1	(14-ounce) can Rotel tomatoes
¾	cup grated Cheddar cheese	½	cup bread crumbs
		3	tablespoons melted butter

Preheat the oven to 350 degrees. Grease a 2-quart casserole dish. In a large skillet, heat the oil over medium heat. Add the garlic and sauté lightly for about 1 minute. Add the zucchini and sauté for 5 minutes. In a small bowl mix the cheese, the oregano, and the basil. With your hands crush the Rotel tomatoes, breaking them into bite-size pieces, and mix them with the seasoned cheese. Beginning with the zucchini, layer the zucchini and the cheese tomato mixture in the prepared dish. Repeat the layering until all ingredients are used, ending with the tomato and cheese mixture. Mix the bread crumbs with the butter and sprinkle on top of casserole. Bake, uncovered, for 30 minutes.

Makes 6 to 8 servings

EGGPLANT AND TOMATO CASSEROLE

This is the eggplant casserole served at Gabriel's.

¼	cup olive oil	½	cup milk
2	large eggplants, peeled and cubed	1	(10¾-ounce) can cream of mushroom soup
1	teaspoon chopped basil	3	large eggs, beaten
2	garlic cloves, minced	1	teaspoon salt
6	tomatoes, peeled, seeded, and chopped or 1 (28-ounce) can tomatoes, well drained and chopped	¼	teaspoon black pepper
		¾	cup cracker crumbs
¼	cup (½ stick) butter	3	tablespoons butter, melted

In a large skillet heat the olive oil over medium heat. Add the eggplant, basil, and garlic and sauté in the olive oil. Turn the heat to low and cover the skillet. Let the vegetables "sweat" for about 15 minutes, stirring occasionally. If you use fresh tomatoes, add them to the eggplant the last 5 minutes of the "sweating" process. (If using the drained canned tomatoes, they will be added later.) Add the butter, milk, soup, eggs, the chopped canned tomatoes (if using the fresh ones, they will already be in the skillet), salt, and pepper. Stir well.

Preheat the oven to 375 degrees. Coat a 14 x 10-inch baking dish with nonstick cooking spray. Add the eggplant mixture. In a small bowl combine the cracker crumbs with the melted butter. Top the eggplant mixture with the buttered cracker crumbs. Bake for 30 minutes. Cover with aluminum foil the last 10 minutes if the cracker crumbs are browning too quickly.

Makes 8 servings

ROASTED CARROT SOUFFLÉ

1½	pounds carrots, sliced		3	large eggs
2	tablespoons butter, melted		¼	cup all-purpose flour
¼	cup light brown sugar		1½	teaspoons baking powder
½	cup (1 stick) butter		¼	teaspoon ground cinnamon
1¼	cups granulated sugar			

Preheat the oven to 450 degrees. In a medium bowl, toss the sliced carrots with the melted butter and the brown sugar, coating well. Transfer the carrot mixture to a roasting pan, spreading the carrots in a single layer. Roast 10 to 15 minutes, or until tender. Stir halfway through cooking to keep any sugar or butter from burning. Remove from the oven.

Reduce the oven temperature to 350 degrees. Lightly grease a 1½-quart soufflé dish. In a food processor, add the carrots, the remaining ½ cup butter, the granulated sugar, eggs, flour, baking powder, and cinnamon. Process until smooth, scraping down the sides. Spoon the carrot mixture into the prepared soufflé dish, leveling the mixture. Bake for 1 hour and 10 minutes, or until set.

Makes 6 servings

SOUTHERN STYLE CREAMED CORN

Customers tell us daily that the creamed corn "tastes like my Nana's corn" or "just like my grandmother's." It is on the menu daily . . . we wouldn't dare rotate it off.

½   cup (1 stick) butter
2   (1-pound) bags frozen white creamed corn

¼   to ½ cup water
    Salt and pepper, to taste
4   to 6 ounces heavy cream

Melt the butter in a medium-size skillet over medium heat. Add the corn and the water, stirring well. Add salt and pepper and the heavy cream. Cook for 20 to 30 minutes, stirring often. The corn is ready when you can't taste the starch in it. Serve hot.

Makes 8 servings

My grandmother (Big Mama) used to make "fried corn." She cut the kernels from the usually white field corn in three steps. With a sharp knife and holding the shucked, cleaned ear of corn over a large bowl, she barely tipped the top off the corn moving from the bottom of the ear to the small end, letting the tips fall into the bowl. Next she cut about half of the kernels off, letting them fall into the bowl. The third step was to scrape what was left on the cob into the bowl. There would be a mix of half kernels, tips, and liquid. She would then run her hand down the ear, squeezing the rest of the liquid from the ear.

Big Mama then sautéed the corn in a large iron skillet with three to four slices of "white meat" (salt pork). Removing the meat when it was crisp, she would pour the corn and liquid into the hot skillet. Then she would cook and stir the corn until it was thick and tasted "done." It no longer tasted like cornstarch. She might add some butter, salt, and pepper to taste. Buying cut, frozen corn allows us to have nearly the same dish with a quarter of the work.

Low-Fat Black Beans over Rice

My friend Saundra Fleming has learned to cook some really good comfort food dishes for her husband, Al. Black beans is one of his favorites.

2	(15-ounce) cans black beans		1½	tablespoons dark brown sugar
2	tablespoons olive oil		2	tablespoons red wine vinegar
1	large onion, chopped		1	cup rice, uncooked
½	green bell pepper, chopped			
2	teaspoons or more minced garlic, according to your taste			

Rinse the black beans, retaining a little of the liquid. In a large saucepan, heat the olive oil over medium heat. Add the onion, green pepper, and garlic, sautéing until the onion is tender and translucent. Add the beans, brown sugar, and red wine vinegar. Cook until the beans are tender. Cook the rice according to the package directions. When ready to serve, spoon the beans over the rice.

Makes 6 servings

RANCHO BEANS

Gail Ré, my friend who helped decorate the stores, shared this delicious and nutritious recipe with me years ago. These are great served with barbecued ribs.

3	tablespoons olive oil	1	(14-ounce) can pinto beans, drained
1½	cups thinly sliced onion	1	tablespoon chili powder
1	shallot, chopped	2	tablespoons cider vinegar
1	cup diced green bell pepper	1	(28-ounce) can Italian style
2	garlic cloves, crushed		tomatoes, chopped
1	(14-ounce) can garbanzo beans,	½	cup firmly packed light brown sugar
	drained	1	teaspoon beef bouillon or ham
1	(14-ounce) can red beans, drained		flavoring

Preheat the oven to 350 degrees. In a large saucepan heat the olive oil over medium heat. Add the onion, shallot, green pepper, and garlic, cooking until the onion is clear. Add the garbanzo beans, red beans, and pinto beans to the onion mixture. Stir well, and then add the chili powder, vinegar, tomatoes, brown sugar, and bouillon or ham flavoring.

Pour the mixture into a 4-quart casserole or a roasting pan. Bake, covered, for 1½ hours. Uncover and bake for 15 minutes longer. Serve hot.

Makes 12 servings

GREEN BEANS

4   to 6 cups water
1/4 green bell pepper, seeded
1   small onion
1 1/2 tablespoons chicken base

2   teaspoons bacon grease
2   teaspoons sugar
2   (28-ounce) cans Italian style green
    beans, drained and rinsed

In a 4-quart stockpot bring the water, bell pepper, onion, chicken base, bacon grease, and sugar to a boil. Cook, uncovered, for 30 minutes. Add the green beans and cook for about 1 hour.

Makes 12 servings

Rancho Beans
(page 152)

CAULIFLOWER BY MARCELLE

Marcelle David of Marietta and her husband, Bill, are widely known for their culinary expertise. Dinner at their home is always eagerly anticipated.

1	head cauliflower, washed and outside leaves cut off	1	cup thinly sliced onion
½	cup mayonnaise	2	tablespoons olive oil
1	teaspoon dry mustard	1	dash Maggi seasoning*
1	cup shredded sharp Cheddar cheese	1	pound French-cut green beans, washed

Place the cauliflower in a pot of boiling water head down for 5 to 10 minutes, then stem down for 5 to 10 minutes. Drain and let cool. In a small bowl mix the mayonnaise and dry mustard together and spread over the cauliflower. Place the cauliflower in a baking dish.

Preheat the oven to 350 degrees. Press the shredded cheese on and around the cauliflower. Bake for 15 to 20 minutes. In a medium skillet, sauté the onion in olive oil until the onion is clear. Add Maggi seasoning and the green beans, sautéing until done to taste. Place the cauliflower on a serving platter. Spoon the green beans around the bottom of cauliflower. Serve hot.

Makes 6 to 8 servings

* Maggi seasoning is often found in the international products section of a grocery store.

TIP: To French-cut fresh beans, cut them in half lengthwise, running the knife down the flat part between the seams of the bean. If the beans are long, cut them at an angle into lengths of about 2 inches.

VIDALIA ONION CASSEROLE

½	cup butter or margarine	½	cup milk
3	pounds Vidalia onions, peeled and sliced		Salt and pepper, to taste
24	saltine crackers (4 ounces), crushed	1	(10¾-ounce) can cream of mushroom soup
2	large eggs	6	ounces Cheddar cheese, grated

Preheat the oven to 350 degrees. Coat a 13 x 9-inch or 14 x 10-inch baking dish with nonstick cooking spray. In a large skillet melt the butter over medium heat. Add the onion, and cook until tender but not browned. Line the prepared dish with the cracker crumbs. In a medium bowl beat the eggs. Add the milk, salt, and pepper. Add the soup and mix well. Layer the onion over the cracker crumbs. Then layer some of the egg mixture. Continue layering the remaining onion and egg mixture, ending with the egg mixture. Sprinkle the grated cheese and additional cracker crumbs over the top. Bake for 20 to 30 minutes, or until brown and bubbly.

Makes 10 to 12 servings

Sweet Potato Casserole

Every Southern family has its own version of this delicious way to eat your vegetables. Gabriel's serves this recipe year-round because it is a customer favorite.

Casserole

4	cups mashed sweet potatoes (we use fresh, roasted, and peeled)
1	cup granulated sugar
1/2	cup firmly packed light brown sugar
1	cup milk
11	tablespoons butter, melted
4	large eggs, beaten just enough to break
2	teaspoons vanilla

Topping

1 1/2	cups chopped pecans or walnuts
2	cups firmly packed dark brown sugar
2/3	cup all-purpose flour
1	cup (2 sticks) butter, melted

Preheat the oven to 375 degrees. Grease a 13 x 9-inch baking dish. In a large bowl combine the sweet potatoes, sugars, milk, butter, eggs, and vanilla. Mix well and pour into the prepared baking dish.

For the topping, in a medium bowl, blend the nuts, brown sugar, and flour. Add the melted butter, and combine, using your hands, to achieve a crumbly mixture. Add more butter if needed. Sprinkle over the casserole and bake for 30 minutes.

Makes 12 servings

HASH BROWN CASSEROLE

One of our customers' favorites, this casserole is on the menu at least every other week.

1   (32-ounce) package frozen shredded
    potatoes, thawed
1   cup (2 sticks) butter, melted, divided
1   (10¾-ounce) can cream of chicken
    soup, undiluted
3   cups (12 ounces) grated American
    cheese

8   ounces sour cream
1   teaspoon salt
½   cup chopped onion
2   cups crushed cornflakes

Preheat the oven to 350 degrees. Spread the thawed potatoes over the bottom of a 13 x 9-inch baking dish. In a medium bowl, combine ½ cup of the melted butter, the soup, cheese, sour cream, salt, and onion, mixing well. Pour the mixture over the potatoes. Top with the cornflakes and drizzle with the remaining ½ cup melted butter. Bake, uncovered, for 45 minutes.

Makes 8 servings

MACARONI AND CHEESE

4	quarts (16 cups) water	3½	cups whole milk
	Pinch of salt	16	ounces Colby cheese, shredded
1	(16-ounce) package elbow macaroni	8	ounces extra-sharp Cheddar cheese
6	tablespoons unsalted butter		Salt and black pepper, to taste
1	teaspoon dry mustard	8	ounces ham, cubed (optional)
6	tablespoons all-purpose flour		About 50 saltines or Ritz crackers
1¾	cups low-sodium chicken broth	2	tablespoons unsalted butter, melted

Preheat the oven to 400 degrees. Coat a 13 x 9-inch baking dish with nonstick cooking spray. In a large stockpot, bring the water to a boil. Stir in a hefty pinch of salt and the macaroni. Cook about 5 minutes, stirring occasionally until the macaroni is al denté. Drain the macaroni and set aside.

Using the same pot after drying it, add the butter and melt on medium heat. Add the dry mustard and the flour, cooking and stirring constantly to make a golden colored roux. Whisk in the chicken broth and milk, simmering 5 to 6 minutes, or until thickened. Remove the mixture from the heat, and stir in the cheeses. Stir until the cheeses are completely melted. Add salt and pepper. Add ham, if desired, for a hearty, main dish meal. Add the pasta to the cheese mixture, stirring to combine and coat all of the pasta. Pour the macaroni mixture into the prepared baking dish. Using a food processor break the crackers into fine crumbs (about 2 cups) or put them in a resealable plastic bag and crush with a rolling pin until they are fine pieces. Add the melted butter. Sprinkle the cracker mixture over the top of the casserole. Bake for 35 to 40 minutes, or until the casserole is bubbling and the cheese melts.

Makes 8 to 10 servings

NOTE: The casserole may be made one day ahead to the point of adding the cracker crumbs. Refrigerate overnight. When ready to bake, remove from the refrigerator about 30 minutes before baking, add the crumbs on top, and bake as directed.

TIP: Al denté is an Italian term meaning "to the tooth" and is used in reference to the degree of doneness of pasta, risotto, or vegetables. The food should be cooked only until it is still slightly chewy when biting into it. It should not be soft and overdone nor have a hard center.

TIP: Roux is a French term to describe a mixture of equal amounts of fat (butter or meat drippings) and flour that are cooked together at the beginning of the recipe before any liquid is added. It is used to thicken sauces. It should be stirred constantly until the liquid is added or it will burn. If it has black, burned specks in it, discard and begin again.

SOUTHERN CORNBREAD DRESSING

I can't imagine Thanksgiving or Christmas without dressing and gravy. In every Southern home, the cornbread dressing will taste a little different. Some Southern cooks include pieces of turkey or chicken, some add more onion, and some prefer a dry dressing. My mother's was, of course, the best I've ever tasted. This is the closest I've come to duplicating it. It's a lot of work, but well worth it. We also serve this casserole during cool weather to accompany roasted chicken.

1	10-inch skillet of cornbread (we use White Lily cornmeal mix)	2½	to 4 cups chicken or turkey broth
3	tablespoons butter	1	cup milk
3	celery stalks, chopped	2	large eggs, beaten
1	large onion, chopped	½	teaspoon salt
9	slices of day-old bread, toasted and crumbled	1	teaspoon poultry seasoning
		½	teaspoon rubbed sage
		¼	teaspoon pepper

Preheat the oven to 350 degrees. Prepare and bake the cornbread according to the package directions. Cool and crumble into a large bowl. In a medium sauté pan, melt the butter over low heat. Add the celery and onion. Cover and "sweat" the vegetables for about 10 minutes, or until tender. Add to the cornbread. Add the toasted bread, 2½ cups broth, the milk, eggs, salt, poultry seasoning, sage, and pepper. The best way to mix this is with your hands, crushing the pieces of cornbread and any pieces of toast to give a mixture with no big lumps. At this point the consistency should be similar to the uncooked cornbread when you poured it into the skillet to bake. If it is too dry, add enough broth to loosen it a little. If it is too thin, break another egg, toast a few more slices of bread and mix them in until you get that uncooked cornbread consistency. (Mother even saved leftover biscuits to use instead of "white bread" toast.)

Spoon the mixture into a greased 13 x 9-inch baking dish. Bake 25 to 35 minutes, or until the mixture is firm and not wet to touch. Serve with giblet gravy (see next page).

Makes 8 to 10 servings

GIBLET GRAVY

An essential recipe to go with Southern cornbread dressing.

	Giblets from a 12- to 15-pound turkey		Turkey drippings (from roasted turkey)
1	medium onion, chopped	½	cup all-purpose flour
2	celery stalks, cut in half	5	to 6 cups turkey stock
¼	teaspoon salt	1	tablespoon chopped fresh sage
6	to 8 cups water or more to cover	1	teaspoon black pepper
	giblets and vegetables	2	hard-boiled eggs, peeled and chopped

Place the uncooked giblets in a 3-quart saucepan except for the liver (set it aside to add later). Add the onion, celery, salt, and water to cover. Bring the water to a low boil. Cover and simmer for about 45 minutes. Add the liver and simmer another 10 to 15 minutes until all the parts are tender. Drain, reserve the broth, and let the giblets cool. (If you don't have 5 to 6 cups of turkey stock left after cooking the giblets, you can substitute a can of chicken broth and 1 cup of water to make 6 cups.) When the giblets are cool, pull the meat from the neck. Chop the neck meat and the giblets. In a large skillet heat the drippings over medium heat. Whisk in the flour, stirring constantly, until it cooks to a golden brown. Add the sage, and heat for 1 minute. Gradually whisk in the turkey stock until blended and smooth. Add ½ cup of the chopped cooked giblets, black pepper, and salt, to taste. Stir until the mixture thickens. Add the chopped eggs.

Makes 8 servings

TIP: Some people are not fond of eating giblets. When I have cooked a smoked turkey breast for the entrée and not had any giblets, I roasted a turkey quarter to get the meat to add to the gravy. However, that doesn't provide you with enough drippings for the gravy, and that is truly where the flavor comes from. Consider roasting a couple of hens just to get poultry drippings, and later use the meat to make chicken salad or chicken potpie for the freezer.

TIP: After roasting the turkey, pour the drippings into a small bowl, scrapping the bottom of the roaster for any sediment. Skim the fat off the top as the drippings, cool, and throw it away. Glean all of the drippings that you can.

My Favorite Food Group— Desserts!

Okay, it is not one of the "official" food groups, but very few people can resist desserts.

I grew up with my paternal grandmother, Big Mama, and she made the best pound cake! I don't have her recipe for it, but I do have memories of the *smell* of a cake baking and the *flavor* of a warm pound cake.

My dad was so spoiled with Big Mama's warm pound cake that he wouldn't eat it cold. He ate it hot out of the oven, or he toasted it and slathered it with butter.

It wasn't just pound cake that Big Mama was famous for. It was also her Sunday dinners after church. If she was cooking and inviting, it meant we were having a ham or fried chicken, creamed corn, green beans, macaroni and cheese, a congealed salad, cornbread made in a black iron skillet, and at least one dessert. She made a strawberry pie that most of us just wanted to take a big spoon and the bowl of pie and go hide. That recipe died with her also. (By the way, I was the last of four granddaughters and I would never have named my grandmother "Big Mama." It in no way described her statue, which is the first thing I picture when I hear that name. It described the size of her heart, spirit, character, work ethic, and the love for her family.)

With two great credentials—a grandmother who was a great cook and my love of desserts—I think I am a good judge of the taste of Southern food. My tastes may not be the most sophisticated, but they have been well exercised. I stick pretty close to the norm and have not tested myself with some of the delicacies that my cousin Paula Deen enjoys. I do, however, feel like I'm an expert on desserts, not necessarily on baking them but in knowing what tastes good and what doesn't. As far as the buying public is concerned, I think that is what is important.

At Gabriel's, the desserts stand the ultimate test: Do they really *taste* good, not just look good? Our bakers are in at 5 AM six days a week to bring flour, sugar, eggs, chocolates, and fruits together to become a concoction worthy of going into the Gabriel's dessert cases. I can't possibly taste every pan of lemon squares that comes out of the oven, but I am often accused of overdoing it on the issue of tasting for "quality control." In other words, I eat my own desserts. I probably don't have the most sophisticated of tastes when it comes to dark chocolates, but give me an authentic tiramisu, a banana cream pie, or a bowl of homemade ice cream, and I believe I can stand with the best of critics.

The taste of Big Mama's German chocolate cake that she made me for my birthdays still hovers in my mind just as I hovered over her kitchen table while she baked for all of us. Little did she or I know that I was in training for what would be one of the most rewarding aspects of my life . . . baking, much less selling, delicious morsels of desserts. The rewarding part is that it's food for our customers that says, "Welcome to our home; we're glad you're here." It also provides a convenience that makes a busy lifestyle just a little less hectic.

Paula Deen's husband, Michael, always reminds me that he wants to get locked in our store one night with red velvet cakes. Paula had me as a guest on one of her Paula's Party episodes, and we baked the red velvet cake. At that time, Bubba, Paula's brother and my cousin, decided that he and his fiancé, Dawn, wanted us to bake their wedding cake for their upcoming marriage in May. The cake was carrot and decorated with hand-rolled sugar pearls and cold-porcelain magnolias—two Southern traditions on a wedding cake for a beautiful, petite, precious Southern bride. For Bubba's groom's cake, we made 250 red velvet cupcakes and put them in Chinese to-go containers. What fun we had being a part of that celebration. Finally, Gabriel's had the opportunity to do something for the Hiers/Deen family.

DESSERTS

The Heart of Gabriel's

VANILLA POUND CAKE

This basic pound cake is good with the Cooked Fudge Frosting (page xx) or Caramel Frosting (page xx).

1	cup (2 sticks) butter, at room temperature	3½	cups all-purpose flour, sifted (we use White Lily)
½	cup shortening	½	teaspoon baking powder
3	cups sugar	½	teaspoon salt
5	jumbo eggs	1	teaspoon pure vanilla extract
		1	cup whole milk

Preheat the oven to 325 degrees. Grease a 15-cup tube pan with a small amount of shortening and sprinkle flour into the bottom and around the sides. Tap out any excess flour. In a large mixing bowl on medium to high speed, beat the butter and the shortening until light and fluffy. Slowly add the sugar at medium speed and then turn to medium high, beating until light and fluffy. Add the eggs, one at a time, beating well after each addition at medium speed.

In a large bowl, sift together the already-sifted flour, the baking powder, and the salt. Add the vanilla to the milk. At a moderately slow speed, add the flour mixture to the butter mixture in four increments, alternating with the milk mixture in three increments. Begin and end with the dry ingredients. Scrape down the sides and the bottom of bowl as you're alternating the flour mixture and the milk. At this point you don't want to over beat. A slow speed is sufficient to just incorporate the flour and milk into the butter mixture. The purpose is to combine the batter just short of having lumps of flour in it.

Pour the batter into the prepared pan, scraping down the sides and bottom of the bowl. If you have the proper-size pan, the batter will fill it two-thirds to three-fourths full. Place the pan in the center of the oven. Bake for approximately 70 to 75 minutes, or until a cake tester inserted in the center comes out clean. A dry crumb can remain on the tester but not wet batter. When the cake is done, remove from the oven and allow it to cool on a wire rack for 10 to 15 minutes.

Gently remove the cake from the pan by inverting onto a rack and then turn right side up onto a cake plate and allow to cool.

Makes 14 to 16 servings

Variations:
- Almond pound cake, add a teaspoon of almond extract instead of vanilla.
- Chocolate pound cake, substitute $1/2$ cup unsweetened cocoa powder for $1/2$ cup of the flour.

TIP: When baking pound cake, do not open the oven door during the first hour.

LEMON-GLAZED POUND CAKE

1   Vanilla Pound Cake (recipe on page 166)

1½ lemons

1   tablespoon butter or margarine, melted

8   ounces confectioners' sugar

Prepare the recipe for the Vanilla Pound Cake. Cool the pound cake in the pan for 10 to 15 minutes. While the cake is cooling, prepare the lemon glaze. Finely zest or finely grate the skin of the lemons and place the zest in a medium-size mixing bowl. Juice the lemons, and add to the bowl with the butter. Sift the confectioners' sugar into the bowl, and combine the ingredients until no lumps remain. Invert the cake onto a rack, and then turn right side up on a cake plate. Pour the lemon glaze over the top of cake and smooth over and down the sides with a spatula or knife, completely covering the cake. Glaze the inside of the opening in the pound cake for even more flavor, using all of the allotted glaze.

Makes 14 to 16 servings

TIP: When frosting or glazing a whole cake on the cake plate, tear four 2- to 3-inch-wide strips of waxed paper. Invert the cake onto a rack and while the cake is upside down place the strips along the bottom of the cake. Turn it right side up onto the serving plate, leaving the strips under the edge. Frost or glaze the cake. Gently pull the strips from under cake leaving your cake plate clean and your cake finished.

COCONUT POUND CAKE

Pound Cake

2	cups sugar
1	cup shortening
4	jumbo eggs
3	cups all-purpose flour
1/2	teaspoon salt
1/2	teaspoon baking powder
1/2	teaspoon baking soda
1	cup buttermilk
2	teaspoons coconut flavoring

Coconut Glaze

2	cups sugar
1	cup water
3	tablespoons butter or margarine
2	tablespoons light corn syrup
2	teaspoons coconut flavoring
4	ounces shredded coconut

Preheat the oven to 350 degrees. Grease and flour a 10-inch tube pan, tapping out any excess flour. (We use a baking spray to prepare our pans.) In a large mixing bowl, beat the sugar and the shortening. Add the eggs, one at a time, mixing well after each addition. Sift together the flour, salt, baking powder, and baking soda. In a small bowl mix the buttermilk with the coconut flavoring. Add the flour mixture in four increments to the sugar mixture, alternating with the buttermilk. Begin and end with the dry ingredients. Pour the batter into the prepared pan and bake for approximately 75 minutes, or until the cake tester inserted near the center of the cake comes out clean. Remove the cake from the oven and punch holes in top of cake with a wooden skewer.

For the glaze, combine the sugar, water, butter, and corn syrup in a small saucepan. Bring to a boil and cook for 2 minutes, stirring constantly. Mix in the coconut flavoring and the coconut. Pour the Coconut Glaze over the cake while the cake is still hot. Let cool 10 minutes and remove the cake from the pan by inverting it onto a cake rack and inverting again onto a cake plate. Let the cake cool completely.

Makes 12 to 14 servings

Peanut Butter Pound Cake

We bake this cake at Gabriel's and frost with the Cooked Fudge Frosting or Chocolate Buttercream Frosting.

1	cup (2 sticks) butter or margarine	1/2	teaspoon baking powder
1	cup crunchy peanut butter	1/2	teaspoon salt
2	cups granulated sugar	1/4	teaspoon baking soda
1	cup firmly packed light brown sugar	1	cup milk
1/2	cup sour cream	1	teaspoon vanilla
5	large eggs	1	cup mini chocolate chips
3 1/2	cups sifted all-purpose flour		

Preheat the oven to 350 degrees. Grease and flour a 15-cup tube pan, tapping out any excess flour. (We use a baking spray to prepare our pans.) In a large mixing bowl, beat the butter, peanut butter, granulated sugar, and brown sugar until light and fluffy. Add the sour cream and the eggs, one at a time, beating after each addition. Scrape down the sides and bottom of the bowl. In a large bowl sift together the flour, baking powder, salt, and baking soda. Put the milk in a small bowl and add the vanilla. Alternately add the flour mixture and the milk to the creamed mixture, beginning and ending with flour. Scrape down the sides and bottom of the bowl. Fold in the mini chocolate chips. Pour the batter into the prepared pan. Bake for 60 to 75 minutes, or until a tester inserted in the center comes out clean. Remove from the oven and cool on wire rack for 10 to 15 minutes. Invert onto a wire rack and invert again onto a serving plate.

Makes 16 servings

PEACH POUND CAKE

We bake Peach Pound Cakes at Gabriel's and sell them whole or by the slice. They don't stay in the case very long.

Pound Cake
1	Vanilla Pound Cake (recipe on page 166)
¼	cup peach brandy
3	drops peach oil
1	cup chopped canned or fresh peaches

Peach Glaze
1	cup sugar
¼	cup peach brandy
½	cup (1 stick) butter
¼	cup water
4	drops peach oil

Preheat the oven to 325 degrees. Grease and flour a 15-cup tube pan, tapping out any excess flour. (We use a baking spray to prepare our pans.) Prepare the pound cake batter according to the directions. While the batter is still in the mixing bowl, stir in the brandy and the peach oil. Pour the batter into the prepared tube pan. Drop the chopped peach pieces on the top of the cake batter and gently swirl the peaches into the batter. Bake for 60 to 75 minutes, or until a tester inserted in the center comes out clean.

Prepare the glaze while the cake is baking. In a small saucepan, stir together the sugar, brandy, butter, water, and peach oil. Bring the glaze to a boil, stirring to melt the sugar and butter. Remove the cake from the oven when it is done, and pour the glaze over the cake. Cool in the pan 15 to 20 minutes on a wire rack. Invert the cake onto the rack and then invert onto a serving plate.

Makes 12 to 14 servings

Rum Pound Cake

Pound Cake

1	Vanilla Pound Cake (recipe on page 166)
¼	cup dark rum

Rum Glaze

1	cup sugar
½	cup (1 stick) butter
¼	cup water
¼	cup dark rum
½	cup chopped pecans

Prepare the batter for the Vanilla Pound Cake. Swirl the rum into the cake batter, mixing well. Bake the pound cake according to the directions in the recipe.

Prepare the glaze while the cake is cooking. In a medium saucepan combine the sugar, butter, water, and rum. Bring to a boil, stirring constantly to melt the sugar. Stir in pecans. When the cake is done, remove from the oven and punch 10 to 12 holes (with a wooden or metal skewer) in top of the cake. Slowly pour the hot Rum Glaze over the cake. The nuts will settle on top and the liquid will be absorbed into the cake. Let the cake cool 10 to 15 minutes in the pan before inverting and then turn over again onto a cake plate. All of the warm glaze should be absorbed into the cake, but be cautious in case there is still warm liquid in the bottom of the cake pan.

Makes 10 to 12 servings

TIP: When inverting a cake with a topping, spray a piece of waxed paper with nonstick cooking spray, and lay the sprayed side down on top of the cake before inverting it. The paper holds the topping in place, and the spray keeps the paper from sticking to the top of the cake.

CHOCOLATE LOVER'S BUNDT CAKE

1 cup (2 sticks) butter or margarine, softened to room temperature
1½ cups sugar
4 jumbo eggs
½ teaspoon baking soda
1 cup buttermilk
2½ cups plain flour, sifted
1½ cups semisweet chocolate mini-morsels, divided

8 ounces sweet baking chocolate, melted and cooled
⅓ cup chocolate syrup
2 teaspoons vanilla extract
2 tablespoons plus 2 teaspoons vegetable shortening, divided
4 ounces white chocolate

Preheat the oven to 300 degrees. Grease and flour a 10-inch Bundt pan with a pan release, tapping out any excess flour. (We use a baking spray to prepare our pans.) In a large mixing bowl beat the butter and sugar with an electric mixer. Add the eggs, one at a time, beating well after each addition. Dissolve the baking soda in the buttermilk, stirring well. Add to the creamed mixture alternately with the flour, beginning and ending with flour. Add 1 cup of the mini-morsels, the melted sweet chocolate, the chocolate syrup, and the vanilla, stirring just until blended. (Do not overbeat.)

Pour the batter into the prepared pan and bake for 85 to 95 minutes, or until the cake springs back when touched. Invert the cake immediately onto a cake plate and let cool completely.

In top of double boiler, melt the remaining ½ cup chocolate mini-morsels and 2 teaspoons of the shortening. Bring the water to a boil. Reduce the heat to low and stir until the chocolate is smooth. Drizzle the chocolate over the cooled cake and allow to set. Repeat the same process with the 4 ounces of white chocolate and the remaining 2 tablespoons shortening, stirring until the mixture is melted and smooth. Remove from the heat. Drizzle the melted white chocolate mixture over the cooled, chocolate-drizzled cake.

Makes 12 to 14 servings

RED VELVET CAKE

2½ cups all-purpose flour, sifted
1 teaspoon baking soda
1 teaspoon cocoa powder
1½ cups vegetable oil
1½ cups sugar
2 jumbo eggs or 3 large

1 teaspoon white vinegar
2 teaspoons vanilla extract
1 ounce red food coloring
1 cup buttermilk
Cream Cheese Frosting
(recipe on page 200)

Preheat the oven to 350 degrees. Grease and flour three 9-inch cake pans, tapping out any excess flour. (We use a baking spray to prepare our pans.) In a medium bowl sift the flour, baking soda, and cocoa powder. In a large bowl combine the oil, sugar, and eggs, mixing well until thoroughly combined. In a small bowl mix the vinegar, vanilla, and red food coloring. Add to the oil mixture, blending well. Add the flour mixture to the oil mixture in three stages, alternating with the buttermilk and beginning and ending with the dry ingredients. Pour equal amounts of batter into the three prepared pans. Tap the pans on the counter surface to level the mixture and release any air bubbles. Bake the cake for 24 to 27 minutes, or until a cake tester inserted near the center comes out clean. Remove the cakes from the oven, place on wire racks, and allow to cool 10 to 15 minutes in the pans. Prepare the Cream Cheese Frosting.

Invert the cake layers onto the cake racks to fully cool. If any layers are significantly higher in the middle, level with a serrated knife to keep the layers from breaking when they are stacked. Put the first cake layer on the cake plate, and spread one-fourth of the cream cheese mixture on the first layer. Place the second layer evenly and securely on top of the frosted layer and spread with an equal amount of frosting. Repeat with the third layer. Use the remaining frosting to cover the sides of the cake.

Makes 14 to 16 servings

TIP: If not frosting the cake as soon as it cools, stack the layers on top of each other, separating with pieces of waxed paper. Wrap airtight with plastic wrap until ready to frost.

VARIATION: To make Red Velvet Cupcakes: Using cupcake liners, prepare a two 12-cup muffin pan. Divide the batter among the twenty-four cups. Bake at 350 degrees for 20 to 24 minutes. Frost with the Cream Cheese Frosting.

Italian Cream Cake

This is one of our best selling layer cakes.

½ cup (1 stick) butter or margarine, softened
½ cup vegetable shortening
2 cups sugar
5 jumbo eggs, at room temperature, separated
2 cups all-purpose flour, sifted
1 teaspoon baking soda
1 cup buttermilk
1 teaspoon vanilla extract
3½ ounces flaked coconut
1 cup chopped pecans
Cream Cheese Frosting (recipe on page 200)

Preheat the oven to 350 degrees. Grease three 9-inch cake pans and line the bottoms with parchment paper. In a large mixing bowl, beat the butter, shortening, and the sugar until light and fluffy. Add the egg yolks, one at a time, beating well after each yolk addition. Scrape down the bottom and sides of the bowl. In a medium bowl sift together the flour and the baking soda. Add to the creamed mixture alternating with the buttermilk, beginning and ending with the dry ingredients. Add the vanilla, coconut, and pecans. In a mixing bowl, beat the egg whites to form a firm peak but not beaten dry. Fold the egg whites into the cake batter. Divide the batter evenly among the three prepared cake pans, tapping them on the counter surface to level the batter and release any air bubbles. Bake for 24 to 27 minutes, or until the cake tester inserted near the center comes out clean. Remove the cakes from the oven, set on a wire rack, and cool in the pans for 10 to 15 minutes. Prepare the Cream Cheese Frosting.

Invert the layers onto the cake racks to continue to cool to room temperature. If any layers are significantly higher in the middle, level with a serrated knife to keep the layers from breaking when they are stacked. Put the first cake layer on the cake plate, and spread one-fourth of the cream cheese mixture on the first layer. Place the second layer evenly and securely on top of the frosted layer and spread an equal amount of frosting. Repeat with the third layer. Use the remaining frosting to cover the sides of the cake. Sprinkle the top of the cake with any extra chopped coconut and pecans.

Makes 14 to 16 servings

IRISH CREAM CHEESECAKE

Crust
10 whole graham crackers
1 ¼ cups pecans
¼ cup sugar
¾ stick butter or margarine, melted

Filling
1½ pounds cream cheese, at room
   temperature
¾ cup sugar

⅓ cup Irish cream liqueur
3 jumbo eggs
1 teaspoon vanilla extract
3 ounces white chocolate

Topping
1½ cups sour cream
¼ cup confectioners' sugar
¾ cup chopped pecans
10 ounces white chocolate, grated

Preheat the oven to 350 degrees.

For the crust: In a food processor, finely grind the graham crackers, pecans, and sugar. Add the melted butter and blend, pulsing until combined. Press the mixture into the bottom of a 9-inch springform pan and 2 inches up the sides. Wrap the outside of the bottom and up the sides of the springform pan with heavy-duty aluminum foil.

For the filling: In a food processor, combine the cream cheese and the sugar. In a medium bowl whisk the liqueur, eggs, and vanilla. Add the liqueur mixture to the cream cheese mixture, and blend in the food processor until smooth. Chop the white chocolate with a chef's knife on a cutting board. Add to the cream cheese mixture in the processor, blending until smooth. Transfer the filling to the crust-lined pan, and place the filled pan in a larger, 3- to 4-inch-deep baking pan. Place the two pans in the oven on the middle rack. Fill the larger pan with about 2 inches of water to create a water bath for the cheesecake. Bake for 1 hour, or until the edges of the cheesecake are puffed and dry and the center is just set. Remove the cheesecake from the oven and cool on a wire rack. When cool, remove the cheesecake from the springform pan.

For the topping: In a small bowl whisk together the sour cream and confectioners' sugar. Spread the topping onto the cheesecake. Sprinkle the outside edges with the chopped pecans, and spread the grated white chocolate over the top. Refrigerate about 6 hours, or until well chilled.

Makes 12 servings

New York Cheesecake

Crust

1	cup graham cracker crumbs
2	tablespoons light brown sugar
½	cup (1 stick) soft butter, at room temperature

Filling

3	(8-ounce packages) cream cheese
1	cup sugar
1	pint (16 ounces) sour cream
8	ounces whipping cream
4	large eggs
2	teaspoons vanilla

Preheat the oven to 350 degrees.

For the crust: Combine the graham cracker crumbs and the brown sugar in a medium bowl. Mix the butter into the crumb mixture (mixing by hand works best), combining well until all the crumbs are wet. Firmly press the crumbs into the bottom and 1 inch up the sides of a 10-inch springform pan. Refrigerate the crust until ready to fill.

For the filling: In a large mixing bowl thoroughly beat the cream cheese and the sugar. Scrape down the sides and bottom of the bowl, and add the sour cream and the whipping cream, combining well. Add the eggs, one at a time, beating after each addition. Add the vanilla flavoring. All ingredients should be incorporated, but do not over beat. Pour the filling into the prepared crust, and bake for 55 to 60 minutes. The outer edges of cheesecake should be firm and set, but the center should be not quite as firm, but still done. Cool on a rack and refrigerate until ready to serve.

Makes 12 servings

TIP: I bake all cheesecakes in a water bath, which adds about 15 minutes to the cooking time but usually prevents the cracking of the top of the cheesecake. See explanation on page xxx.

PRALINE CHEESECAKE

Crust
1   cup ground toasted pecans
1/4   cup firmly packed dark brown sugar
1/4   cup butter or margarine, melted
3   tablespoons all-purpose flour

Cheesecake
3   (8-ounce) packages cream cheese, at room temperature
3/4   cup firmly packed dark brown sugar
1   tablespoon cornstarch
5   ounces evaporated milk
3   tablespoons praline liqueur
3   jumbo eggs

Topping
1   (8-ounce) carton sour cream
3   tablespoons sugar
1   large egg yolk
1   teaspoon vanilla extract
1/2   cup Praline Pecans, chopped coarsely (recipe on next page)

Preheat the oven to 350 degrees. Grease a 9-inch springform pan.

For the crust: In a food processor combine the toasted pecans, brown sugar, butter, and flour. Process just until the ingredients are combined. Press the crust mixture into the bottom of the prepared springform pan. Bake for 15 minutes. Remove from the oven and place on a wire rack to cool completely. Reduce the oven temperature to 325 degrees.

For the filling: In the large bowl of an electric mixer, combine the cream cheese, brown sugar, and cornstarch. Mix well, scraping down the sides and bottom of the bowl. Add the evaporated milk, liqueur, and eggs, mixing just until combined. Pour into the cooled crust and bake for 1 hour. Remove the cheesecake from the oven and increase the oven temperature to 400 degrees.

For the topping: In a bowl, whisk together the sour cream, sugar, egg yolk, and vanilla. Blend well. Pour over the cheesecake and return the cheesecake to the oven. Bake for 5 minutes. Turn off the oven and let the cheesecake stand in the oven for 30 minutes. Leave the oven door slightly ajar. Remove from the oven and refrigerate.

Just before cutting and serving, cover the top of the cheesecake with Praline Pecans.

Makes 12 servings

PRALINE PECANS

Pi-kahn' or pee'-kan as my cousin Paula calls them—are a Southern staple. We are in love with their taste and crunch they add to almost any dish. For me they enhance desserts, vegetables, starches, and salads—and are equally delicious as a snack or appetizer. We use these praline pecans on our pumpkin pie, praline cheesecake, and on a green salad with blue cheese and several fresh fruits.

2	tablespoons butter or margarine	$\frac{1}{2}$	cup chopped pecans
$\frac{1}{4}$	cup firmly packed dark brown sugar		

In a small skillet melt the butter and brown sugar over medium heat. Add the pecans, stirring until bubbly. Remove from the heat and pour onto aluminum foil. When the pecans are cool, crumble into small pieces. Sprinkle the topping over desserts or salads.

Makes enough to cover 1 pumpkin pie or 1 praline cheesecake

YELLOW LAYER CAKE

This layer cake is the basis for several of Gabriel's very popular desserts . . . Fresh Strawberry Cake, Caramel Layer Cake, and our traditional American Birthday Cake with Chocolate Frosting.

½	cup vegetable shortening	½	teaspoon salt
½	cup (1 stick) butter	½	cup milk
2	cups sugar	½	cup buttermilk
4	large eggs, separated	¼	cup cream
3	cups all-purpose flour, sifted before measuring (we use White Lily)	1	tablespoon vanilla Caramel Frosting (recipe on page 198) or frosting of choice
2	teaspoons baking powder		

Preheat the oven to 350 degrees. Lightly grease and flour the bottom center of three 9-inch round cake pans, tapping out any excess flour. (We use a baking spray to prepare our pans. Line the bottoms with parchment paper, spray the parchment paper, and the sides of the pans.) In a large bowl of an electric mixer, beat the shortening, butter, and sugar, blending until fluffy. Scrape down the sides and bottom of the bowl. Add the egg yolks, one at a time, mixing well after each addition. In a separate large bowl, sift together the flour, baking powder, and salt. Set aside.

In a medium bowl combine the milk, buttermilk, cream, and vanilla. In three additions, add the flour mixture alternately with the milk mixture to the creamed mixture. Begin with flour and end with flour, scraping down the bottom and sides of the bowl after each addition. Blend evenly, but do not overmix. Using a whisk attachment on the mixer, whip the egg whites until they will hold a peak. Using a rubber spatula, gently fold the whipped egg whites into the cake batter in three additions. Divide the cake batter among the prepared cake pans. Gently tap the cake pans on the counter or tabletop to level out the batter in the pan. Bake for 22 to 26 minutes, or until a cake tester inserted near the center comes out clean. The top of the cake layers should have baked to a golden color. Cool the cake pans on a wire rack for 15 to 20 minutes. Remove the cake from the pans onto a wire rack to finish cooling. Brush the layers with simple syrup (see tip).

Pour a little less than one-third of the frosting on the first layer, spreading evenly with an icing spatula to the outside edges. The caramel sets up fairly quickly on the cake so work as efficiently as possible. Place the second layer on top of caramel and firmly seat it. Repeat the process on the second layer as you did on bottom layer. If the caramel becomes too stiff to spread, put a cup or so in a microwavable cup and heat in 20-second bursts, stirring between bursts until it is once again creamy. Repeat the procedure with the third layer. Spread the remaining frosting around the sides by keeping it in front of the spatula and pulling it around the cake in one direction, not back and forth.

Makes 14 to 16 servings

TIP: For the Yellow Layer Cake, we use a simple syrup to brush the layers before frosting. In a small heavy saucepan combine 1 cup sugar and 1 cup water. Bring to a boil, stirring constantly. Reduce the heat, and simmer for 3 minutes. Allow the syrup to cool. With a pastry brush apply a light coating of the simple syrup on the unfrosted cake layers. Any leftover syrup will keep in the refrigerator for up to two weeks for future use. Simple syrup is also good to sweeten iced tea.

TIP: For layer cakes, if the layers are higher in the middle, level them with a serrated knife before frosting.

FRESH STRAWBERRY CAKE

This cake is found at Gabriel's all year long. It is our most requested wedding cake and our best-selling retail cake.

1   Yellow Layer Cake (recipe on   Cream Cheese Frosting (recipe on
      page 182)   page 200)
1½   cups chopped, washed, and hulled
      fresh strawberries, divided

Grease and flour three 9-inch round cake pans, tapping out any excess flour. (We use a baking spray to prepare our pans.) Prepare the Yellow Layer Cake batter according to the recipe. Before placing in pans to bake, fold in ³/₄ cup of the strawberries. Divide the batter evenly among the prepared pans. Bake according to the recipe directions. Remove from the oven and let cool on a wire rack. When cool, if not frosting immediately, stack the layers with waxed paper between them and wrap tightly in plastic wrap.

When ready to frost, prepare the Cream Cheese Frosting according to the recipe directions. Fold in the remaining ³/₄ cup strawberries. Place the first cake layer on a cake plate and spread with one-fourth of the frosting. Place the second layer evenly and securely on top of the frosted layer and spread with an equal amount of frosting. Repeat with the third layer. Use the remaining frosting to cover the sides of the cake. Keep the cake refrigerated in a closed container until ready to serve. Any leftover cake should be kept refrigerated in a closed container.

Makes 14 to 16 servings

German Chocolate Cake

This was the cake that I always wanted my grandmother to make for my birthday. It is one of our most popular cakes at the store. I still love having a piece of German chocolate cake.

Cake
½ cup boiling water
4 ounces Baker's German Sweet Chocolate
½ cup (1 stick) butter or margarine
2 cups sugar
4 jumbo eggs, separated
1 teaspoon vanilla extract
2 ½ cups all-purpose flour, sifted
½ teaspoon salt
1 teaspoon baking soda
1 cup buttermilk

Frosting
3 large egg yolks, slightly beaten
1 cup evaporated milk
1 cup sugar
½ cup (1 stick) butter or margarine, cut into pieces
1 teaspoon vanilla
1 cup chopped pecans
7 ounces coconut (Baker's Angel Flake or equivalent)

Preheat the oven to 350 degrees. Grease and flour three 9-inch baking pans, tapping out any excess flour. (We use a baking spray to prepare our pans.) In a small bowl, melt the chocolate in the boiling water and let cool. In an electric mixer, beat the butter and sugar until light and fluffy. Add the egg yolks, one at a time, beating well after each. Blend in the vanilla and chocolate. Sift the flour, salt, and baking soda. Add to the creamed mixture, alternating with the buttermilk, beginning and ending with dry ingredients. In a mixing bowl beat the egg whites until soft peaks form. Fold the egg whites into the batter. Pour even amounts of batter into the prepared pans. Bake for 24 to 27 minutes, or until the layers test done when a cake tester placed in the center comes out clean. Remove the cakes from the oven, and let cool in the pans 10 minutes. Remove the layers from the pans by inverting onto wire cake racks. Let stand until fully cooled.

Prepare the frosting: In a medium bowl whisk the egg yolks and the milk. Add the sugar and butter to the yolks and milk and put in the top of a double boiler. Bring the water in the bottom pan to a boil. Lower the heat and cook over medium heat, stirring occasionally, until the mixture thickens (coating the back of a spoon when stirred). Add the pecans and coconut, and mix well by hand.

Place the first cake layer on a cake plate and spread one-fourth of the frosting on the first layer. Place the second layer evenly and securely on the top of the filled layer and spread an equal amount of filling on the second layer. Repeat with the third layer. Use the remaining frosting to cover the sides of the cake.

Makes 14 to 16 servings

TOASTED COCONUT CAKE

For coconut lovers, this recipe is a good alternative to a fresh coconut cake, which usually has a time-consuming 7-minute cooked frosting.

3	cups flaked coconut, toasted and divided	2	cups sifted all-purpose flour
1	cup (2 sticks) butter or margarine, at room temperature	1	teaspoon baking powder
		1	teaspoon baking soda
2	cups sugar		Pinch of salt
1	tablespoon vanilla extract	1	cup buttermilk
4	large eggs, at room temperature, separated	¼	teaspoon cream of tartar
			Cream Cheese Frosting (recipe on page 200)

Preheat the oven to 325 degrees. Spread the coconut on a foil-lined baking sheet, and toast for 12 minutes, stirring every 5 minutes. The color should be golden not brown. Cool and set aside. In the bowl of an electric mixer, beat the butter and sugar until fluffy and light. Add the vanilla, beating until smooth. Add the egg yolks, one at a time, beating well after each addition. Scrape down the bowl. In a large bowl sift the flour with the baking powder, baking soda, and salt. Add the flour mixture to the butter mixture, alternating with the buttermilk in three additions, beginning and ending with the flour mixture. Scrape down the bowl. Add 1 cup of the toasted coconut, using the Stir speed on the mixer. In a separate bowl beat the egg whites until frothy. Add the cream of tartar, beating until stiff peaks form. Gently fold the egg whites into the batter.

Lightly grease and flour the bottom center of three 9-inch round cake pans, tapping out any excess flour. (We use a baking spray to prepare our pans. Line the bottom with parchment paper and spray the parchment paper and sides of the pans with the spray.) Divide the batter evenly among the pans, smoothing and leveling the top of the layers with a spatula. Bake for 25 to 30 minutes, or until a cake tester inserted near the center comes out clean. Cool for 10 minutes in the pans. Invert cake layers onto wire racks and cool to room temperature. When cool, wrap well if not filling and frosting immediately.

To frost, prepare the Cream Cheese Frosting and fold in 1 cup of the toasted coconut. Place the first cake layer on a cake plate, and spread with one-fourth of the frosting. Place the second layer evenly and securely on top of the frosted layer and spread with an equal amount of frosting. Repeat with the third layer. Use the remaining frosting to cover the sides of the cake. Press the remaining cup of toasted coconut into the sides and top of the cake. This cake does not need to be refrigerated.

Makes 14 to 16 servings

CHOCOLATE FUDGE CAKE WITH PECANS

The cinnamon in this sheet cake gives it a wonderful flavor.

Cake

2   cups all-purpose flour
2   cups sugar
½   cup (1 stick) butter or margarine
½   cup vegetable shortening
4   tablespoons cocoa powder
1   cup water
½   cup buttermilk or sour milk
1   teaspoon baking soda
1   teaspoon cinnamon

2   large eggs, slightly beaten
1   teaspoon vanilla

Chocolate Frosting

½   cup (1 stick) butter or margarine
7   tablespoons milk
4   tablespoons cocoa powder
1   pound confectioners' sugar
1   teaspoon vanilla
1   cup chopped pecans

Preheat the oven to 400 degrees. Grease and flour a 13 x 9-inch baking pan, tapping out any excess flour. (We use a baking spray to prepare our pans.) In a large bowl sift together the flour and sugar. In a 2-quart saucepan combine the butter, shortening, cocoa powder, and water. Bring to a rapid boil. Pour the hot mixture over the flour mixture, stirring until well blended. Add the buttermilk, baking soda, cinnamon, eggs, and vanilla, mixing until blended.

Pour the batter into the prepared pan. Bake for 30 minutes, or until a cake tester comes out clean when inserted in the center.

Prepare the frosting about 5 minutes before the cake is finished baking. Combine the butter, milk, and cocoa powder in a 4-quart saucepan. Bring to a boil. Remove the mixture from the heat and stir in the confectioners' sugar and the vanilla, whisking until the sugar is completely combined. Add the nuts.

Remove the cake from the oven, and place on a wire rack. Immediately pour the warm Chocolate Frosting over the cake. The frosting will not be stiff, so it will run to the sides of the pan. Use a spatula to gently spread the frosting over cake as evenly as possible.

Makes 12 to 14 servings

TIP: When a customer orders this cake from Gabriel's, we turn the hot cake out on a cake board before frosting and just "deal" with the frosting running off the sides of the cake. As it cools, we use a spatula to scoop it up and on top of the cake. At home, put the cake plate inside a cookie sheet to catch the frosting running off the sides of the cake.

Irish Cream Cheesecake (page 178)

CHOCOLATE FLOURLESS CAKE

We sell this flourless chocolate cake at Gabriel's. We spread a thin layer of chocolate ganache on the top and sides and garnish with a handful of white and dark chocolate curls. It is a perfect dessert for gluten-intolerant sweets lovers.

1½	cups (3 sticks) butter	4	ounces unsweetened chocolate, chopped into small pieces
6	ounces semisweet chocolate, chopped into small pieces	1½	cups sugar
6	ounces white chocolate, chopped into small pieces	9	large eggs
		1	to 2 tablespoons cocoa powder

Preheat the oven to 300 degrees. Grease and flour a 9-inch round cake pan with 2-inch-high sides, tapping out any excess flour. (We use a baking spray to prepare our pans.) In a medium-size microwave-safe bowl or over a water bath over low heat, melt the butter, semisweet chocolate, white chocolate, and unsweetened chocolate. Stir constantly until completely melted and smooth. If using a microwave, melt the chocolate in bursts, stirring to be sure the chocolates don't burn.

In the container of a food processor, combine the sugar and the melted chocolates. Process for 1½ minutes. Add the eggs and continue to process for another 1½ minutes. Pour the batter into the prepared pan. (This cake will not rise when baked, so if the batter is near the top of the pan it will not overflow.) Bake in a water bath for 1 hour and 5 minutes. Remove from the oven and let cool on a rack for 10 to 20 minutes. Refrigerate until firm. When ready to serve, run a thin sharp knife around the outside edge of cake and invert onto a serving plate. Lightly dust the top of the cake with cocoa powder.

Makes 8 servings

NOTE: Use real chocolate pieces, not an imitation, with this recipe. It is well worth the difference in cost.

TIP: If a cake doesn't easily release from the pan when inverted, try tapping on the bottom of the pan, dipping the bottom of the pan into warm water, or heating the bottom of the pan with a hand-held torch.

DOUBLE-FUDGE CHOCOLATE CAKE

This is the chocolate layer that we use for all of our chocolate cakes except for the German chocolate cake.

Cake
1 ½ cups hot, brewed coffee
3 ounces semisweet chocolate
¾ teaspoon vanilla
3 cups sugar
4 large eggs, at room temperature
¾ cup vegetable oil
2 ½ cups sifted all-purpose flour
1 ½ cups cocoa powder
2 teaspoons baking soda

¾ teaspoon baking powder
1¼ teaspoons salt
1½ cups buttermilk

Double-Fudge Frosting
13½ ounces semisweet chocolate chips
¾ cup (1½ sticks) butter
½ cup light corn syrup

Preheat the oven to 350 degrees. Grease and flour three 9-inch round cake pans, tapping out any excess flour. (We use a baking spray to prepare our pans.) In a small bowl pour the hot coffee over the semisweet chocolate, stirring with a whisk to evenly melt the chocolate. Whisk in the vanilla. In a large mixing bowl mix the sugar, eggs, and oil. Add the melted chocolate mixture. In another large bowl sift together the flour, cocoa powder, baking soda, baking powder, and salt. Add the flour mixture and the buttermilk alternately in three to four increments to the sugar mixture, beginning with the flour and ending with the flour. Distribute the batter evenly in the prepared pans. Bake for 25 to 27 minutes, or until a cake tester inserted near the center comes out clean. Remove from the oven and cool 10 minutes in the pans. Remove the layers from the pans by inverting onto cake racks, and cool completely.

For the frosting: In a medium bowl set over a pan of almost simmering water, melt the chocolate and butter, whisking to combine well. Stir in the corn syrup, mixing well. Remove the bowl from heat and let cool, stirring occasionally. Place the first cake layer on a cake plate, and spread with one-fourth of the frosting. Place the second layer evenly and securely on top of the frosted layer and spread with an equal amount of frosting. Repeat with the third layer. Use the remaining frosting to cover the sides of the cake.

Makes 14 to 16 servings

CARROT CAKE

2 cups sugar
1¼ cups vegetable oil
4 jumbo eggs
3 cups finely shredded carrots
2½ cups sifted all-purpose flour
2¼ teaspoons baking soda

2 teaspoons ground cinnamon
1 cup chopped pecans, divided
Cream Cheese Frosting (recipe on
page 200)

Preheat the oven to 350 degrees. Grease and flour three 9-inch round cake pans, tapping out any excess flour. (We use a baking spray to prepare our pans.) In large mixing bowl combine the sugar and oil, beating thoroughly with an electric mixer. Add the eggs, one at a time, and beat well after each addition. Add the carrots and mix well. In a large bowl sift together the flour, baking soda, and cinnamon. Add the dry ingredients to the wet ingredients, and mix well. Stir in ½ cup of the pecans. Pour even amounts of batter into the three prepared pans. Bake for 24 to 27 minutes, or until a cake tester inserted near the center of layers comes out clean. Remove the cake from the oven, and let cool 10 minutes in pan. Remove the layers from the pans by inverting onto cake racks. Let stand until fully cooled.

Make the Cream Cheese Frosting, adding the remaining ½ cup chopped pecans. Place the first cake layer on a cake plate, and spread with one-fourth of the frosting. Place the second layer evenly and securely on top of the frosted layer and spread with an equal amount of the frosting. Repeat with the third layer. Use the remaining frosting to cover the sides of the cake.

Makes 14 to 16 servings

VARIATION: To make Carrot Cake Cupcakes: Using cupcake liners, prepare two 12-cup muffin pans. Divide the batter among the twenty-four cups. Bake at 350 degrees for 20 to 24 minutes. Frost with the Cream Cheese Frosting.

Hummingbird Cake

2 cups sugar
3 cups all-purpose flour, sifted
1 teaspoon baking soda
1 teaspoon salt
1 teaspoon ground cinnamon
3 jumbo eggs
1 cup vegetable oil

1½ teaspoons vanilla extract
1 (8-ounce) can crushed pineapple
1½ cups chopped pecans, divided
2 cups ripe bananas, mashed
Cream Cheese Frosting (recipe on page 200)

Preheat the oven to 350 degrees. Grease and flour three 9-inch round cake pans, tapping out any excess flour. (We use a baking spray to prepare our pans.) In a large mixing bowl combine the sugar, flour, baking soda, salt, and cinnamon. Add the eggs and the oil. Stir, by hand, until all dry ingredients are moistened. Stir in the vanilla, pineapple, 1 cup of the pecans, and banana. Pour equal amounts of batter into the prepared pans, tapping the pans on the countertop to level and release air bubbles. Bake for 28 to 30 minutes, or until a cake tester inserted near the center comes out clean. Remove the cake from the oven and let cool in the pans for 10 minutes. Remove from pans by inverting onto cake racks. Let stand on the racks until completely cooled.

To frost, prepare the Cream Cheese Frosting, adding the remaining ½ cup pecans. Place the first cake layer on a cake plate and spread with one-fourth of the frosting. Place the second layer evenly and securely on top of the frosted layer and spread with an equal amount of frosting. Repeat with the third layer. Use the remaining frosting to cover the sides of the cake.

Makes 14 to 16 servings

Cooked-Fudge Frosting

This old-fashioned cooked fudge frosting that we use at the store is one of the most requested chocolate frostings. We tried many recipes to get to this workable, great tasting one. The key ingredient to its "setting up" is the corn syrup.

3	cups sugar	11	tablespoons butter
½	cup cocoa powder	3	tablespoons light corn syrup
¾	cup whole milk	1½	teaspoons vanilla

Sift the sugar and cocoa powder into a heavy-bottom 4-quart saucepan. Whisk in the milk, butter, and corn syrup. Over medium to medium-high heat, bring the mixture to a full boil, whisking and stirring the bottom and sides of the pan. Cook 1 minute. Remove from the heat and add the vanilla. Let cool for a few minutes, and then pour into the large mixing bowl of an upright mixer, beating at a medium speed until the mixture loses its gloss and begins to thicken to a spreading consistency.

Makes enough frosting for three 9-inch round cake layers

TIP: The most difficult part of getting the frosting to set up is deciding how long to beat it after cooking and determining when it is ready to spread. If it hardens too much, reheat in the microwave until it gets to a spreading consistency. Adding liquid if it's too firm will not alleviate the problem but only add to it.

CARAMEL FROSTING

Family and friends who understand the labor of cooked caramel frosting will think you're a fabulous baker when you present a cake with this frosting. Those who don't know what you've been through will simply compliment you and look forward to their next invitation. Either way, you come away looking and feeling accomplished. This frosting is sometimes referred to as cooked or burned sugar caramel.

3 cups sugar, divided
¾ cup evaporated milk
¾ cup (1 ½ sticks) butter

1 tablespoon white corn syrup
1 teaspoon vanilla

Bake the cake layers, and cool completely before starting the frosting. Have all ingredients for the frosting pre-measured. Place ½ cup of the sugar in a heavy saucepan (see Tip) on top of the stove over medium heat. As the sugar begins melting, shake the pan to keep it evenly spread over the bottom but not on the sides of the pan. If uneven melting (browning) occurs, stir the sugar with a wooden spoon to keep it melting evenly. Use the spoon to break up any chunks of the sugar. The sugar should be melted to a color a little lighter than the skin of an almond.

Quickly, but carefully, pour in the evaporated milk. Add the remaining 2½ cups sugar, the butter, and the corn syrup, stirring to mix well. The milk addition stops the melting of the sugar and produces a quick reaction in the pan and may appear to boil furiously. This is why we use a saucepan instead of a shallow iron skillet. Attach a candy thermometer to the side of the saucepan and continue to boil until the temperature reaches 248 degrees. Pour the mixture into a large mixing bowl and add the vanilla. Using a heavy-duty upright mixer, beat the caramel mixture until it loses it gloss and is a creamy consistency, not still liquid. Stop the mixer once or twice while beating and scrape down the sides and bottom of the bowl after the mixture has thickened and starts to lose its gloss. You are simply cooling the mixture to the proper temperature. No amount of beating will produce a spreadable frosting that has been undercooked (less than 248 degrees).

Makes enough frosting for three (9-inch) round cake layers

TIP: Many veteran chefs use an iron skillet for this recipe. We get the best results by using an All-Clad stainless-steel 4-quart saucepan or a Dutch oven. The pan used is very important as the frosting is cooked at moderately high temperatures and a flimsy pan will allow the sugar to burn. You will also need a candy thermometer, a wooden spoon, a frosting spatula, and a heavy-duty electric mixer.

TIP: If the caramel becomes too stiff to spread when frosting your cake, put a cup or so in a microwavable cup and heat in 20-second bursts, stirring between bursts until it is once again creamy.

CREAM CHEESE FROSTING

¾ cup (1½ sticks) butter or margarine
1½ (8-ounce) packages cream cheese,
    at room temperature
1½ (16-ounce) packages confectioners'
    sugar, sifted

1 cup chopped pecans, lightly toasted
    (optional)
1½ teaspoons vanilla

In a large mixing bowl combine the butter and cream cheese, mixing well. Add the confectioners' sugar in increments, scraping down the bottom and sides of the bowl once or twice between additions. Add the pecans and vanilla. Mix well.

Makes enough frosting for three 9-inch round cake layers or a large pound cake with leftover frosting

VANILLA BUTTERCREAM FROSTING

We use this frosting at Gabriel's for our wedding cakes and special occasion cakes. This frosting can be made two to three days ahead of time. Store any leftover frosting in the refrigerator and rewhip when ready to use.

5	sticks butter	1 1/2	(16-ounce) packages confectioners' sugar, sifted
1 1/4	cups vegetable shortening	1	tablespoon vanilla flavoring

In a large mixing bowl, with the paddle attachment, beat the butter and shortening until soft. Scrape down the sides and bottom of the bowl. Add the confectioners' sugar in two to three increments. Scrape down the bowl again. Add the vanilla and whip for about 5 minutes. When ready to frost a cake, place one layer flat side up on a cake plate, and with an offset spatula or knife, spread enough of the frosting to cover the layer to the edges. Repeat the same process with the second and third layers, spreading the frosting on the sides of the cake after adding the third layer.

Makes 10 cups frosting

CHOCOLATE BUTTERCREAM FROSTING

2   (1-pound) boxes plus ½ cup
     confectioners' sugar, sifted
1   cup cocoa powder, sifted
5   sticks butter

1¼   cups vegetable shortening
¾   cup (6 ounces) milk
2   teaspoons vanilla flavoring

Sift together the confectioners' sugar and the cocoa. Set aside. In a large mixing bowl, with the paddle attachment, beat the butter and shortening until soft. Scrape down the sides and bottom of the bowl. Add the sugar/cocoa mixture in two to three increments. Scrape down the bowl again. Add the milk and vanilla and whip for about 5 minutes. When ready to frost a cake, place one layer flat side up on a cake plate, and with an offset spatula or knife, spread enough of the frosting to cover the layer to the edges. Repeat the same process with the second and third layers, spreading the frosting on the sides of the cake after adding the third layer.

The frosting can be made two to three days ahead of time. Store any leftover frosting in the refrigerator and rewhip when ready to use.

Makes 12 cups frosting, enough to frost two 3-layer 9-inch round cakes

TOLLHOUSE PIE

A wonderful restaurant in Charleston, South Carolina, 82 Queen, gave me several recipes in September 1989, the week prior to Hurricane Hugo hitting the city. My dearest friend Carole Simpson has a condominium on Isle of Palms just off the coast of Charleston, and I am fortunate enough to get to visit often. We ended one visit to Isle of Palms a couple of days prior to Hugo. There was so much destruction from the hurricane that it was more than a year before we could return. Little did I know when I tucked this recipe into my book that I would one day be baking this pie to sell.

2	large eggs	1	cup chopped walnuts
½	cup all-purpose flour	1	(9-inch) pie shell, partially baked
½	cup sugar	1	cup whipped whipping cream or ice
½	cup firmly packed brown sugar		cream (optional)
1	cup (2 sticks) butter, melted and cooled to room temperature		Walnut halves (optional)
1	(6-ounce) package semisweet chocolate chips		

Preheat the oven to 325 degrees. In a large bowl, beat the eggs until foamy. Beat in the flour, sugar, and brown sugar until well blended. Blend in the melted butter. Stir in the chocolate chips and the chopped walnuts. Pour the mixture into the partially baked pie shell, and bake for 1 hour or until set. Remove the pie from the oven. Let cool on a wire rack or serve warm. If desired, serve with whipped cream garnished with a walnut half or with ice cream. The pie may be reheated in the microwave to serve warm after cooling.

Makes 1 pie (6 to 8 servings)

KEY LIME PIE

This is the recipe we serve at Gabriel's.

1   (14-ounce) can sweetened
    condensed milk
3   large egg yolks
½   cup fresh or bottled key lime juice
1   (9-inch) graham cracker pie crust,
    baked

2   cups whipping cream
¼   cup confectioners' sugar
    Fresh strawberry slices, for garnish

Preheat the oven to 350 degrees. In a large mixing bowl combine the condensed milk, egg yolks, and lime juice, blending well. Pour into the graham crust, and bake for 10 minutes. Let stand 10 minutes before refrigerating. When ready to serve, beat the whipping cream in a mixing bowl. As the cream begins to thicken, slowly add the confectioners' sugar, whipping until peaks form. Fill a piping bag with the freshly whipped cream and pipe a wide border of whipped cream around the outside edge of the pie. Or place a dollop of whipped cream on each piece as you cut it. Garnish with fresh strawberry slices for extra color.

Makes 1 pie (8 to 10 servings)

Chocolate Fudge Pie

We sell this pie at Gabriel's . . . it's a winner! We serve it with a dollop of ganache and chocolate curls. It's great with whipped cream, too.

1/3	cup plus 1 tablespoon cocoa powder	2	teaspoons vanilla
2	cups sugar	3	large eggs, beaten
6½	tablespoons butter, melted	1	(9-inch) deep-dish pie shell
1	(8½-ounce) can evaporated milk		

Preheat the oven to 350 degrees. In a large bowl sift together the cocoa powder and sugar. Add the melted butter, the evaporated milk, and the vanilla. Add the eggs and mix well. Pour into the pie shell and bake for 1 hour.

Makes 1 pie (6 to 8 servings)

CREAM PIES

¾	cup sugar	3	cups milk
¼	cup plus 2 teaspoons cornstarch	1½	tablespoons butter
⅛	teaspoon salt	1½	teaspoons vanilla
3	large egg yolks, beaten (if adding a meringue topping, save the egg whites)	1	(9-inch) deep-dish pie shell, baked

In a heavy saucepan combine the sugar, cornstarch, and salt. Whisk the ingredients together well. In a medium bowl combine the egg yolks and milk. Whisk into the sugar mixture in the saucepan. Cook over medium heat, stirring constantly, until the mixture thickens and begins to boil. Boil 1 minute, stirring constantly. Remove from the heat and stir in the butter and the vanilla. Pour the mixture immediately into the pie shell. See options below for variety of cream pies and for whipped cream or meringue toppings.

Makes 1 pie (6 to 8 servings)

BANANA WHITE-CHOCOLATE CREAM PIE: Melt 2 ounces of white chocolate with 1 teaspoon vegetable shortening and spread it over the bottom of the cooked pie shell. Slice a banana and place the slices on top of the white chocolate. Cover the bananas with the cooked vanilla pie filling. Cover the top with waxed paper, and chill in the refrigerator. When chilled, top with whipped cream. Sprinkle 2 ounces grated white chocolate over the whipped cream.

BUTTERSCOTCH CREAM PIE: Substitute ¾ cup firmly pack dark brown sugar for the white sugar. Reduce the vanilla to ¾ teaspoon and add ¾ teaspoon butter flavoring.

CHOCOLATE CREAM PIE: Follow the above recipe, adding ¼ cup cocoa powder when combining the sugar, cornstarch, and salt. Add 4 ounces semisweet chocolate chips when adding the butter to the cooked mixture.

COCONUT CREAM PIE: Follow the main recipe, adding $^1/_2$ cup flaked coconut and 1 teaspoon coconut flavoring to the cooked mixture. Sprinkle $^1/_4$ cup toasted coconut on top of the whipped cream topping or meringue topping.

WHIPPED CREAM TOPPING:

1   cup whipping cream
$^1/_2$ cup sifted confectioners' sugar

Cover the pie with waxed paper, and let cool 30 minutes. When cool, refrigerate until firm. Beat the whipping cream until foamy. Gradually add the confectioners' sugar, beating until soft peaks form. Remove the waxed paper and spread the whipped cream over the top of the pie and to the edges to seal. Chill until ready to serve.

EGG WHITE MERINGUE:

3   large egg whites, at room temperature

$^1/_2$ teaspoon cream of tartar
$^1/_4$ cup plus 2 tablespoons sugar

In a large bowl beat the egg whites and cream of tartar at high speed for 1 minute. Gradually add the sugar, one tablespoon at a time. Beat the egg whites 2 to 4 minutes, or until stiff and the sugar dissolves. Do not beat until dry peaks form. Spread the meringue over the hot pie filling, sealing to the edge of the pastry. Bake the pie at 350 degrees for 10 to 12 minutes, or until the meringue is golden brown. Let cool to room temperature and refrigerate.

PUMPKIN PIE

This is the best pumpkin pie I have ever eaten. It is the recipe we use at the store.

1	(9-inch) pie shell	1½	teaspoons ground ginger
1	(15-ounce) can unsweetened		Pinch of cloves
	pumpkin puree		Pinch of nutmeg
3	large eggs, at room temperature		Pinch of salt
1	cup firmly packed light brown sugar	2	tablespoons dark rum
2	tablespoons unsalted butter, melted	2	teaspoons vanilla
	and cooled	¼	cup confectioners' sugar
2½	cups heavy cream, divided	¼	cup Praline Pecans (recipe on
⅓	cup sour cream		page 181)
1½	teaspoons ground cinnamon		

Preheat the oven to 450 degrees. Partially bake the pie shell according to the
package directions. In the large bowl of an electric mixer, whisk the pumpkin,
eggs, brown sugar, melted butter, 1½ cups of the heavy cream, sour cream,
cinnamon, ginger, cloves, nutmeg, salt, dark rum, and vanilla for 2 to 3 minutes.
Pour into the shell. Bake for 10 minutes, and then reduce the oven temperature
to 300 degrees. Continue baking for 35 to 45 minutes. Cool to room temperature,
and refrigerate until ready to serve. With the whisk attachment of an electric
mixer, whip the remaining cup of heavy cream on a high speed until the cream
starts to froth. Gradually add the confectioners' sugar and whip on high until the
cream stands in peaks. Either spoon or pipe the whipped cream around the
edges of the pie and garnish with Praline Pecans.

Makes 1 pie (6 to 8 servings)

BLUEBERRY NUT PIE

This recipe, like the Tollhouse Pie, was once served at 82 Queen in Charleston, South Carolina.

1 (8-ounce) package cream cheese, at room temperature
3 cups confectioners' sugar
2 (9-inch) pie shells, baked

1 cup chopped walnuts, divided
1 (21-ounce) can blueberry pie filling
2 cups whipping cream, whipped

In a mixing bowl beat the cream cheese and confectioners' sugar until well blended. Spread evenly in the two pie shells. Use $^3/_4$ cup of the walnuts to sprinkle over the cream cheese in both pie shells. Divide the blueberry filling in half and spread half over each pie. Top the pies with whipped cream and the remaining walnuts.

Makes 2 pies (12 to 16 servings)

PECAN BARS

One of my favorite desserts, these bars sell well at Gabriel's.

Crust

1	cup (2 sticks) butter, very cold (I actually keep this butter in the freezer)
½	cup confectioners' sugar
1	large egg
3	cups all-purpose flour
½	teaspoon salt
1	teaspoon lemon zest

Filling

1	cup (2 sticks) butter
½	cup honey
1	cup plus 2 tablespoons dark brown sugar
¼	cup granulated sugar
¼	cup heavy cream
5	cups pecan pieces

Preheat the oven to 350 degrees. Grease and flour two 13 x 9-inch baking pans, tapping out any excess flour. (We use a baking spray to prepare our pans.)

For the crust: In a food processor, pulse the butter and confectioners' sugar just until mixed into coarse pieces. Add the egg, flour, salt, and lemon zest. Pulse until the mixture looks like cornmeal (still dry). Divide the mixture evenly between the two prepared pans. With your fingertips, press the crust evenly into the bottom and to the edges of the pan. Work quickly as the heat from your fingers will start to melt the butter. Bake the crust for 20 minutes.

For the filling: In a 4-quart saucepan, bring the butter, honey, and sugars to a boil, boiling for 1 minute. Remove from the heat and add cream and pecans.

Pour the filling into the crust, spreading evenly. Bake for 15 minutes or until bubbly. Remove from the oven and cool on a wire rack. Cut the mixture in each pan into 24 pieces. Pecan bars may be frozen in an airtight container for up to two weeks or frozen for up to 30 days.

Makes 48 bars

WHITE CHOCOLATE AND PECAN BROWNIES

3 ounces unsweetened chocolate, chopped	3 large eggs
¾ cup (1½ sticks) unsalted butter, at room temperature	¾ cup all-purpose flour
½ cup firmly packed light brown sugar	6 ounces white chocolate, cut into ½-inch pieces
½ cup granulated sugar	1 cup pecans, chopped
	Confectioners' sugar, for garnish

Preheat the oven to 350 degrees. Line the bottom of a 13 x 9-inch baking pan with parchment paper or aluminum foil. Grease and flour the foil and sides of pan, tapping off any excess flour. In top of a double boiler over simmering water, stir the unsweetened chocolate until melted. Remove the chocolate from over the water and cool. In a large mixing bowl, beat the butter until light and fluffy. Gradually add the sugars, beating until well blended. Mix in the melted chocolate. Add the eggs, one at a time, and beat after each addition until blended. Mix in the flour. Fold in the white chocolate pieces and the pecans. Spread the batter in the prepared pan. Bake for 20 minutes, or until a tester inserted near the center comes out with just a few crumbs attached. Cool the brownies in the pan on a wire rack.

When ready to serve, cut around the sides of the pan to loosen the brownies. Turn out onto a cutting board and peel off the liner. Cut into 2- to 3-inch squares. Turn right side up, dust with confectioners' sugar, and arrange on a serving plate. The brownies may also be frosted with fudge icing, but do this before removing them from the pan.

Makes 24 to 32 servings

Crème de Menthe Brownies and Lemon Bars

LEMON BARS

Crust

2	cups all-purpose flour
1/2	cup confectioners' sugar
3/4	cup (1 1/2 sticks) butter or margarine, very cold and cut into slices

Filling

1/2	cup all-purpose flour
1/2	teaspoon baking powder
4	large eggs
2	cups sugar
1/2	teaspoon grated lemon peel
1/3	cup lemon juice
	Confectioners' sugar, for garnish

Preheat the oven to 350 degrees. Grease and flour a 13 x 9-inch baking pan, tapping out any excess flour. (We use a baking spray to prepare our pans.)

For the crust: In a food processor combine the flour, 1/2 cup confectioners' sugar and butter pieces. Pulse in short spurts until the mixture becomes coarse crumbs. Press evenly into the prepared pan. Bake for 20 to 22 minutes.

For the filling: In a large mixing bowl combine the flour and baking powder. Set aside.

In a separate large mixing bowl combine the eggs, sugar, lemon peel, and lemon juice. Stir the dry ingredients into the wet ingredients, and mix well. Pour the filling over the baked crust and bake for 26 to 28 minutes, or until browned and set. When cooled, cut into 32 pieces and sift a light coat of confectioners' sugar over them before serving.

Makes 32 bars

Crème de Menthe Brownies

Although these dessert bars have several steps of preparation, they are fantastic and well worth making.

Brownie Layer
4 ounces unsweetened baking chocolate
1 cup (2 sticks) butter or margarine
4 large eggs
2 cups sugar
½ teaspoon salt
1 teaspoon vanilla
1 cup sifted all-purpose flour

Filling
½ cup (1 stick) butter or margarine
4 cups confectioners' sugar
¼ cup whipped cream
¼ cup crème de menthe liqueur

Topping
6 ounces semisweet chocolate chips
¼ cup (½ stick) butter or margarine

Preheat the oven to 350 degrees. Grease a 13 x 9-inch baking pan.

Prepare the brownie layer: Melt the unsweetened chocolate and the butter in the top of a double boiler. Cool slightly. In a large mixing bowl beat the eggs until light and fluffy. Beat in the sugar. Add the salt, vanilla, flour, and the melted chocolate mixture. Beat for 1 minute. Pour into the prepared pan and bake for 30 to 35 minutes. Do not overbake. Cool on a wire rack.

Prepare the filling: In a large bowl beat the butter and sugar. Gradually add the whipped cream and the crème de menthe. The mixture will be light and fluffy. Spread the filling over the cooled base and refrigerate for 1½ hours.

Prepare the topping: In the top of a double boiler, melt the chocolate and butter over medium heat, stirring to combine well.

Spread the topping with a spatula evenly over the chilled brownies. Chill. When ready to serve, cut into 32 pieces. Keep refrigerated in an airtight container. These brownies can be frozen for up to 30 days.

Makes 32 brownies

TIP: When cutting these brownies, dip your knife into hot water, dry the knife and cut. Repeat with each cut. This will keep the filling from smearing the top of the brownies.

FROSTED BUTTERSCOTCH BLONDIES

Blondies

1½ cups all-purpose flour
½ teaspoon baking powder
¼ teaspoon salt
1 cup (2 sticks) unsalted butter
1¾ cups firmly packed light brown sugar
3 large eggs
1½ teaspoons vanilla

Caramel Frosting

¾ cup heavy cream
½ cup firmly packed light brown sugar
¼ cup granulated sugar
4 large egg yolks
6 tablespoons unsalted butter
  Pinch of salt
1 teaspoon vanilla
1 cup sweetened flaked coconut
¾ cup chopped pecans, toasted

Preheat the oven to 350 degrees. Grease and flour a 13 x 9-inch baking pan, tapping out any excess flour. (We use a baking spray to prepare our pans.)

For the blondies: In a small bowl, whisk together the flour, baking powder, and salt. In a large mixing bowl, beat the butter and brown sugar at medium speed until light and fluffy, about 3 minutes. Add the eggs, one at a time, beating well after each addition. Beat in the vanilla. At a low speed of the mixer, add the dry ingredients to the wet ingredients in three additions, stirring until just blended. Using a rubber spatula, spread the batter evenly in the prepared pan. Bake for 35 to 40 minutes, or until golden and a cake tester inserted near the center of the blondies comes out clean. Cool on a wire rack.

For the frosting: In a heavy medium saucepan, combine the cream, sugars, egg yolks, butter, and salt. Cook over medium heat, stirring constantly with a wooden spoon, for about 12 minutes, or until the sugar dissolves and the mixture thickens. Do not boil. The mixture is thick enough when it coats the back of the spoon. Strain the mixture into a large bowl, pressing it through a sieve with a rubber spatula. Stir in the vanilla, coconut, and toasted pecans. Set aside to cool.

When the blondies are cool, use a spatula to spread the Caramel Frosting evenly over them. Cover the pan and refrigerate for 30 minutes. Cut the blondies into 24 pieces. They do not need to be refrigerated.

Makes 24 blondies

CHOCOLATE CHIP OATMEAL COOKIES

1   cup (2 sticks) butter or margarine
1   cup vegetable oil
1   cup firmly packed light brown sugar
1   cup granulated sugar
1   large egg
2   teaspoons vanilla extract
3½ cups all-purpose flour
1   teaspoon baking soda
½   teaspoon salt
1   teaspoon cream of tartar
1   cup regular oats, uncooked
1   cup rice cereal
1   (12-ounce) package semisweet
    chocolate morsels
¾   cup chopped pecans

Preheat the oven to 375 degrees. Grease two cookie sheets. In a large bowl beat the butter and oil. Gradually add the sugars, blending and beating at medium speed of an electric mixer. Add the egg and the vanilla. In a large bowl combine the flour, baking soda, salt, and cream of tartar. Gradually add to the creamed mixture, mixing well. Stir in the oats, rice cereal, chocolate morsels, and chopped pecans. Drop the batter by teaspoonsful on the prepared cookie sheets. Bake for 7 minutes and turn rack 180 degrees in the oven. Bake for another 7 minutes and check edge of cookie for browning. Cookie should start to take on a darker color around the edges. Cool on wire racks.

Makes 10 dozen cookies

OATMEAL RAISIN COOKIES

1	cup (2 sticks) butter or margarine	1	teaspoon cinnamon
1	cup firmly packed light brown sugar	½	teaspoon salt
½	cup granulated sugar	3	cups rolled oats
2	large eggs		(not quick-cooking oats)
1	teaspoon vanilla	1	cups raisins
1½	cups all-purpose flour		
1	teaspoon baking soda		

Preheat the oven to 350 degrees. In a large mixing bowl beat the butter and sugars until creamy. Add the eggs and the vanilla. In a medium bowl sift together the flour, baking soda, cinnamon, and salt. Add to the creamed mixture. Stir in the oats and raisins, mixing well. Use an ice cream scoop to place the cookie dough onto nonstick cookie sheets. Bake for 10 to 12 minutes. Let cool on the cookie sheets for about 10 minutes, and then move to a baking rack to cool thoroughly.

Makes 3 dozen cookies

TIP: You can use a variety of sizes of ice cream scoops to dip your cookies. Experiment with different sizes to come up with a size that's right for your family. Dip your scoop into a container of hot water between each scoop and the dough will release. At Gabriel's we bake our cookies in our convection oven with the blower on. If the recipe calls for a conventional oven baking temperature, we reduce the temperature 20 to 25 degrees and turn the cookie sheet around in the oven after half of the baking time to give a more evenly baked cookie.

SOFT GINGER COOKIES

My daughter, Stephanie, gave me this recipe. It is her husband Vern's favorite cookie. We serve these at Gabriel's.

2¼	cups all-purpose flour	¾	cup butter, margarine,
¾	teaspoon cinnamon		or vegetable shortening
2	teaspoons ginger ground	1½	cups sugar, divided
1	teaspoon baking soda	1	large egg
½	teaspoon cloves, ground	¼	cup molasses
¼	teaspoon salt		

Preheat the oven to 350 degrees. Line two baking sheets with parchment paper. In a medium bowl combine the flour, cinnamon, ginger, baking soda, cloves, and salt. Set aside. In a large mixing bowl on a low speed, beat the butter to soften. Gradually add 1 cup of the sugar, beating until fluffy. Add the egg and the molasses, beating well. Stir the flour mixture into the sugar mixture. Shape the batter into 1½-inch balls. Roll each ball in the remaining sugar. Place on the prepared baking sheets. Bake for about 10 minutes. Cool on the pan for 10 to 15 minutes before transferring to a wire rack.

Makes 2 dozen cookies

CHOCOLATE TOFFEE COOKIE

One of Gabriel's Desserts best-selling cookies, Chocolate Toffees are a little tricky to mix, so follow the directions exactly.

½	cup all-purpose flour	1¾	cups firmly packed dark brown sugar
1	teaspoon baking powder	4	large eggs
¼	teaspoon salt	1	tablespoon vanilla extract
1	pound semisweet chocolate, chopped	7	ounces chocolate toffee pieces
¼	cup (½ stick) unsalted butter	1	cup chopped walnuts

Preheat the oven to 350 degrees. In a small bowl whisk together the flour, baking powder, and salt. Melt the chocolate over a double boiler, stirring constantly, over low heat, or melt in the microwave oven in a microwave-safe bowl. Stir at 30-second intervals until completely melted. Melt the butter in the microwave oven in a microwave-safe bowl. (The temptation here for an experienced baker is to melt the chocolate and the butter together. For some reason this doesn't work well in this recipe. More often than not the chocolate will seize.)

In a large bowl using an electric mixer, whisk the sugar and eggs for about 5 minutes. The volume will increase significantly and the mixture will thicken. Add the melted chocolate and then the melted butter to the egg mixture. Add the flour in increments to the chocolate mixture. Scrape down the sides and bottom of the bowl to incorporate all of the chocolate. Fold in the toffee pieces and the walnuts. Chill the batter about 30 minutes, or until firm. (If you let this cookie dough chill over night, it gets really stiff. At Gabriel's we then let it sit out about 30 minutes before we try to scoop it.)

With an ice cream scoop that holds about 2 ounces, drop the cookies onto a parchment-lined cookie sheet or on a nonstick cookie sheet, spacing them 3 inches apart. Bake for about 7 minutes and then turn the pan and bake for 7 or 8 minutes longer. Cool on baking sheets as the cookies will be very soft coming out of the oven.

Makes 1½ to 2 dozen

TIP: My friend Trish Elliott buys these from Gabriel's and microwaves them about 15 seconds and serves them with a scoop of vanilla ice cream. Top with a cherry, if desired. Softening the ice cream and placing it between two cookies and then frosting makes a great ice cream sandwich.

White-Chocolate Macadamia Nut Cookies

½	cup unsalted butter or margarine, softened	2	cups all-purpose flour
½	cup vegetable shortening	1	teaspoon baking soda
¾	cup firmly packed light brown sugar	½	teaspoon salt
½	cup granulated sugar	6	ounces white chocolate, chopped in ¼- to ½-inch pieces
1	large egg	7	ounces macadamia nuts, coarsely chopped
¾	teaspoon vanilla		

Preheat the oven to 350 degrees. In a large mixing bowl beat the butter and shortening until soft and well blended. Slowly add the sugars, beating until well mixed. Add the egg and vanilla. Scrape down the sides and bottom of the bowl. In a medium bowl, blend the flour, baking soda, and salt. Gradually add to the butter mixture. Stir in the white chocolate and the nuts. Drop by heaping tablespoons (or use a small ice cream scoop) onto a nonstick cookie sheet or onto a parchment-lined baking pan. Bake for 12 to 14 minutes, or until lightly browned around the edges. Cool for 5 to 10 minutes on the cookie sheet and then remove to a wire rack to cool completely.

Makes 36 to 40 cookies

TIP: When I'm baking at home and need to blend my dry ingredients, I sift my measured flour and other dry ingredients onto a piece of waxed paper to keep from having another bowl to wash.

CHEWBILEE COOKIES

A top-selling cookie at the store

2	pounds (8 sticks) unsalted butter	3	pounds all-purpose flour
1	pound 5 ounces sugar (about 3 cups)	1¼	tablespoons baking soda
1	pound 5 ounces light brown sugar (about 3¼ cups)	2	pounds (32 ounces) white chocolate chunks (use real white chocolate)
8	large eggs	20	ounces dried cranberries or cherries
1	tablespoon vanilla	16	ounces walnut pieces

Preheat the oven to 350 degrees. In a large mixing bowl beat the butter and sugars. Add the eggs, one at a time. Scrape down the bottom and sides of the bowl to thoroughly combine. Add the vanilla. In a large bowl sift together the flour and the baking soda. In increments add the flour to the sugar mixture, scraping down sides and bottom of bowl and mixing just enough to combine. Fold in the white chocolate chunks, cranberries or cherries and the walnuts, stirring well enough to evenly distribute them. Drop by heaping tablespoons (or use a small ice cream scoop) onto a nonstick baking sheet or onto a parchment-lined baking pan. Bake for 12 to 14 minutes, or until lightly browned around the edges. Cool 5 to 10 minutes on a cookie sheet and then remove to wire rack to cool completely.

Makes 80 (3-ounce) cookies

TIP: Cookie doughs, once the flour is added, are never beaten like a cake batter. They are mixed just enough to combine the dry ingredients.

BLACK AND WHITE CHOCOLATE-
COVERED CHERRY COOKIES

1	(10-ounce) jar maraschino cherries, drained (reserving juice) and cut in half	1	cup sugar
		1	large egg
$1\frac{1}{2}$	cup all-purpose flour	$1\frac{1}{2}$	teaspoons vanilla
$\frac{1}{2}$	cup cocoa powder	6	ounces semisweet chocolate morsels
$\frac{1}{4}$	teaspoon salt	$\frac{1}{2}$	cup condensed milk
$\frac{1}{4}$	teaspoon baking powder	4	ounces white chocolate chunks, melted
$\frac{1}{4}$	teaspoon baking soda		
$\frac{1}{2}$	cup butter or margarine, softened	1	to 2 teaspoons vegetable shortening

Preheat the oven to 350 degrees. Drain the cherries in a colander, reserving the juice. In a medium mixing bowl, sift together the flour, cocoa powder, salt, baking powder, and baking soda. In a large mixing bowl, beat the butter and sugar on a low speed of the mixer until fluffy. Add the egg and the vanilla, beating well. Gradually add the dry ingredients to the creamed mixture. Stir until well blended. Shape the dough into 1-inch balls and place on an ungreased cookie sheet. Press down the centers with your thumb. Place half a cherry in the center of each cookie. In a small saucepan heat the semisweet chocolate pieces and the condensed milk until the chocolate is melted. Stir 4 teaspoons of the cherry juice into the melted chocolate mixture. Drop about 1 teaspoon of chocolate mixture over each cherry to cover it. (Thin the frosting with additional cherry juice if necessary.) Bake the cookies for 10 minutes. Cool on a wire rack.

In a double boiler or in a microwave-safe bowl, melt the white chocolate and 1 teaspoon of the vegetable shortening over low heat, stirring to blend well. Spoon about $\frac{1}{2}$ teaspoon melted white chocolate over the top of each cookie, letting in run in a free-form down the side of the chocolate-covered cherry. If the white chocolate mixture thickens, quickly add another teaspoon of shortening and reheat.

Makes 36 cookies

TIP: When adding the white chocolate garnish to the baked cookie, fill a small pastry bag fitted with a small pastry tip and drizzle the white chocolate over the cookie. The secret to using a pastry tip is to be sure to thoroughly melt and combine the white chocolate and shortening so there are no lumps that won't fit through the tip but also being careful not to burn the white chocolate. White chocolate melts at a lower temperature than dark chocolate, so it will burn if you use a High microwave temperature and use the same time as you would a dark chocolate.

Pumpkin Cookies

My good friend and coworker Pam Addicks gave me this recipe.

Cookies

2	cups vegetable shortening
2	cups sugar
1	(15-ounce) can pumpkin puree (2 cups)
2	large eggs
2	teaspoons vanilla
4	cups all-purpose flour
1	teaspoon salt
1	teaspoon baking soda
2	teaspoons baking powder
2	teaspoons cinnamon
1	teaspoon allspice
1	teaspoon nutmeg
2	cups raisins
1	cup chopped pecans or walnuts

Orange Frosting

1	pound confectioners' sugar
1	(8-ounce) package cream cheese, at room temperature
¼	cup orange juice concentrate

Preheat the oven to 350 degrees. In a large mixing bowl beat the shortening and the sugar until light and fluffy. Add the pumpkin, eggs, and vanilla, mixing well. In a large bowl sift together the flour, salt, baking soda, baking powder, cinnamon, allspice, and nutmeg. Add the dry ingredients to the creamed ingredients, mixing well. Fold in the raisins and nuts. Drop the batter by teaspoonful onto a nonstick cookie sheet. Flatten a little with the back of the spoon and bake for 14 minutes.

While the cookies are baking, prepare the frosting. In a medium mixing bowl, combine the confectioners' sugar and the cream cheese. Add enough orange juice concentrate, a little at a time, to make the frosting an easy-to-spread consistency. (You won't necessarily use all of the concentrate.) When the cookies are done, spread the frosting over the top of the warm cookie with a spatula. Remove the cookies to a baking rack and let cool.

Makes 5 dozen

Tip: Using a sifter is the most effective way to mix and distribute evenly the dry ingredients in a recipe. Lots of trained culinary people use a fine sieve and shake the dry ingredients into a bowl. I guess I just have really fond memories of my grandmother cranking that sifter. It meant something great would be coming out of the oven. She could have no more baked without a sifter than without an oven.

FRUITCAKE COOKIES

You don't have to be a fruitcake lover to like them. They were a Christmas standard at our house when our daughters were growing up.

1	(15-ounce) box white seedless raisins	5	to 6 cups chopped pecans
1	pound crystallized pineapple, chopped into 1-inch chunks	1	cup firmly packed light brown sugar
1½	to 2 cups (10-ounce box) pitted dates, chopped	3	large eggs
		1	cup (2 sticks) butter
1	pound candied cherries, chopped into ¼-inch pieces	1	teaspoon cinnamon
		1	teaspoon baking soda
3	cups all-purpose flour, divided	½	cup milk

Preheat the oven to 325 degrees. Line a cookie sheet with parchment paper. In a large bowl combine the raisins, pineapple, dates, and cherries. Add $^1/_2$ cup of the flour, mixing well to disburse the flour among the fruit. Add the pecans to the fruit mixture and refrigerate until ready to add to the cookie dough. In a large mixing bowl with an electric mixer, beat the butter and brown sugar. Add the eggs, one at a time, beating after each addition. Sift the remaining $2^1/_2$ cups flour, the cinnamon, and the baking soda into another bowl. Add the dry ingredients to the creamed mixture, alternating with the milk.

Fold, by hand, the fruit and nut mixture into the cookie dough, distributing the fruit and nuts well. Drop by teaspoonsful onto the prepared cookie sheet. Bake for 16 to 18 minutes, or until browned slightly around the bottom edge of the cookies. Cool on a wire rack. Store in an airtight container.

Makes 96 (2-inch) cookies

DIVINITY CANDY

This was my Grandmother Howell's recipe. I remember watching her make divinity. I could hardly wait until it was finished.

4	cups sugar		3	large egg whites
1	cup light corn syrup		1	teaspoon vanilla
¾	cup water		1	cup broken pecans

In a 4-quart heavy-duty saucepan, stir together the sugar, corn syrup, and water until completely combined. Cook over medium heat without stirring until the temperature on a candy thermometer reaches 255 degrees. (A small amount dropped into cold water forms a hard ball.) While the sugar is cooking, stiffly beat the 3 egg whites with an electric mixer. Slowly pour the hot sugar over the egg whites in a thin stream until all the sugar is in the egg whites. Continue beating the mixture until it holds its shape and loses its gloss. Add the vanilla and the nuts. Quickly drop teaspoonsful onto waxed paper.

Makes 96 pieces

Pralines

Judy Watts shared this recipe with me. It was handed down to her from her Aunt Polly, whose family a couple of generations ago lived in New Orleans, a city renowned for its pralines. Judy and I made them one Sunday afternoon in December. It was just the first of many batches she makes during Christmas to give to her friends. I intend to ask Judy how to get on her gift list.

4	cups sugar		Pinch of salt
2	cups whole milk	2	teaspoons vanilla
2	tablespoons butter	4	cups pecans, cut into medium-size
1	teaspoon baking soda		pieces

In a high-sided, heavy-duty saucepan, combine the sugar, milk, butter, baking soda, and salt. Cook the mixture over low heat, *without* stirring, until the temperature reaches 231 degrees or the cooking mixture forms a soft ball when dropped from a spoon into cold water. (We tested the mixture several times before the liquid rolled into and semi held its shape in a ball.)

While the sugar mixture is cooking, spread waxed paper on the countertop. When the sugar reaches the soft-ball stage, immediately remove the pan from the heat and add the vanilla and pecans, stirring quickly and thoroughly. The mixture will begin to thicken and become glossy. The change in sheen is small and the thickening occurs quickly, so work quickly, dropping by tablespoonsful onto the waxed paper. The pralines will set and cool on the paper in 10 to 15 minutes. When cool, wrap individually in plastic wrap. Store in an airtight container for up to two weeks.

Makes 2 dozen pralines

ALMOND BUTTER CRUNCH

Bobbi Jessen made this for many years and gave as Christmas gifts. She gave me the beautiful gift of her friendship and later shared this recipe. Sheilah King now continues Bobbi's tradition of making and giving Almond Butter Crunch to her friends.

There are many steps to this candy—cooking, cooling, and melting. Don't be intimated by it. It is quite easy as long as you follow the steps. You can complete each step of cooling, do another task, and pick it up again for the next step because the candy will hold at a cool room temperature and wait for the next application. It is well worth it, but you will have acquaintances angling to get on your gift list once they taste it.

	Vegetable shortening	¼	cup (3 tablespoons) water
1	cup (2 sticks) unsalted butter	2	cups roasted, diced almonds, divided
1⅓	cups sugar	2	(8-ounce) milk chocolate candy
1	heaping tablespoon light corn syrup		bars, chopped and divided

Lightly grease a 13 x 9-inch glass or metal baking pan with vegetable shortening. In a 1-quart saucepan over low heat, melt the butter until almost fully liquid. Add the sugar, corn syrup, and water, stirring to combine. Continue to cook over low heat, stirring often with a wooden spoon, until the mixture reaches the hard-crack stage on a candy thermometer (300 to 305 degrees). The bulb of the thermometer must be submerged in the mixture but not touching the bottom of the pan or it will break in the candy. At 280 degrees pay close attention as the temperature rises rapidly at this point. At 300 to 305 degrees, add 1 cup of the almonds, stirring to combine, and immediately remove the pan from the heat. Pour the mixture evenly into the prepared pan, tilting to spread the toffee to the edges of the pan. With a spatula, press the cooked toffee down to an even height around the pan. Set the pan aside to allow it to cool. The bottom of the pan will be very hot so protect the surface you set it on if necessary. (At this point the mixture may be refrigerated to cool but will need to be brought out of the refrigerator and come completely to room temperature before going to the next step. The toffee needs to always be at room temperature before each new step.) The toffee is cooled completely when it has lost its sheen.

While the toffee is still cooling in the pan, begin melting half the chocolate in top of double boiler over simmering hot water, stirring to smooth out any lumps. When the chocolate is melted and the toffee is at room temperature, gently invert the toffee pan and turn it out onto a larger baking sheet that is lined with waxed paper. (Ideally the toffee should not break, but it is not uncommon for it to break in half at this point. It won't interfere with the remaining steps if it does). With a paper towel, gently pat the toffee to remove any shortening residue that may be on it. When the chocolate is melted and smooth, spread it evenly and to the edge of the toffee, using a spatula or knife to level. Sprinkle the remaining 1/2 cup diced almonds evenly on top of the chocolate. The chocolate will not be completely covered with almonds. Let the chocolate slightly cool and lose a little of its gloss. With your fingertips, lightly press the almonds into the chocolate and refrigerate until firm.

Remove the toffee from the refrigerator and gently invert the candy (almond and chocolate side down) onto another waxed paper-lined baking sheet. In the same double boiler, melt the remaining chocolate pieces over simmering hot water, stirring to smooth out the chocolate. Spoon the melted chocolate over the brittle, spreading it evenly to the edges. Press another 1/2 cup almonds into the chocolate. Refrigerate again until firm. Gently break the chocolate candy into pieces. Store in an airtight container in the refrigerator or at room temperature. Candy will keep for up to 1 month.

Makes 2¼ pounds candy

TIP: Sheilah buys her almonds (roasted and diced) in bulk from www.almondplaza.com instead of purchasing small packages in the grocery store. She also watches for special sales in the grocery store on the chocolate bars. The candy bars will keep in the pantry until you're ready to use them.

SPANISH CUSTARD

Marie Fernandez Kleber shares her family recipe for Spanish custard, which is actually the same as a flan. The Fernandez family owned and operated The Trio Restaurant in Marietta for many years.

8	large eggs	2	cups sugar, divided
2	quarts (8 cups) whole milk	1	tablespoon vanilla

Preheat the oven to 325 degrees. In a blender mix the eggs, milk, 1 cup of the sugar, and the vanilla. Set aside. In a heavy-duty 2-quart saucepan on medium heat, cook the remaining cup of sugar, stirring constantly with a wooden spoon until the sugar is completely melted and is a medium brown color. Pour the melted sugar into 12 (6- to 8-ounce) custard cups, dividing it among them. The sugar will harden immediately.

Pour the custard mix over the caramelized sugar. Place the custard cups in 14- x 10-inch glass or metal baking pans. Fill the baking pans with enough cold water to come halfway up sides of custard cups to create a water bath. Bake for 55 to 60 minutes, or until the custard is set.

Makes 12 servings

TIP: When using a water bath, put the pans in the oven and then add the water. It prevents spilling and getting any water in the custard and/or cheesecake on the way to the oven.

APPLE GALETTE

This is the French name for a rustic apple tart. It's easily assembled and can be made with plums or peaches. It's really good served hot with ice cream or whipped cream.

1	(9-inch) pie crust, at room temperature	½	teaspoon cinnamon
1	cup all-purpose flour	2½	to 3 apples
2	cups sugar	2	to 3 tablespoons apricot preserves
¼	teaspoon nutmeg	1	to 2 tablespoons water
		2	tablespoons rock sugar

Preheat the oven to 350 degrees. Unfold the pie crust, and place on a baking sheet.

In a medium bowl mix the flour, sugar, nutmeg, and cinnamon. Place the dry ingredients on the unfolded pie crust. Peel and slice the apples into thick slices. Place the apple slices on top of the dry mixture. Fold in about 1 to 1½ inches of the pie crust sides toward the center of the galette. Bake for 45 minutes.

In a small saucepan mix the preserves and the water. Whisk briskly over low heat, bringing the ingredients to a boil. Remove from the heat. Brush the sides and top of the galette with the apricot glaze and sprinkle with the rock sugar.

Makes 1 pie (6 to 8 servings)

BREAD PUDDING

My friend Kathy Pilcher served this one night at her home. I thought it was the best bread pudding I'd ever had!

Pudding
1	loaf French bread
1	quart (4 cups) milk
3	large eggs, beaten
2	cups sugar
1	tablespoon vanilla
1	teaspoon cinnamon
1	cup raisins (optional)
3	tablespoons butter

Whiskey Sauce
½	cup (1 stick) butter
1	cup sugar
1	large egg, beaten
¼	cup bourbon

In a large bowl break the bread into bite-size pieces. Pour the milk over it to soak for 1 hour. Preheat the oven to 375 degrees. Grease a 13 x 9-inch baking pan with butter.

Add the beaten eggs and sugar to the soaked bread. Stir in the vanilla, cinnamon, and the raisins, if desired. Pour the bread mixture into the pan and bake for 1 hour. Watch well during the last 15 minutes and remove from the oven earlier if the dish begins to dry out.

While the pudding is baking make the Whiskey Sauce. In the top of a double boiler, melt the butter and sugar, stirring well. Whisk in the egg, mixing well; remove from the heat and cool. Add the bourbon and pour over the hot pudding.

Makes 12 generous servings

NOTE: In an effort to be somewhat cholesterol conscious, Kathy sometimes uses skim milk and egg substitute.

TIRAMISU

A cooked custard makes the difference in this authentic Italian dessert as opposed to using a flavored whipped-cream filling. At Gabriel's we also bake our own ladyfingers. You'll probably find it much less labor intensive if you buy them. Buy the crusty ones, not the soft ones. They can be found at a specialty foods store.

1	cup sugar	½	cup Kahlúa
½	cup Marsala wine	1½	packages ladyfingers
6	large egg yolks	1½	cups whipping cream, whipped
1	pound mascarpone cheese, at room temperature	½	cup confectioners' sugar, more or less to taste
1½	cups hot water	4	ounces semisweet chocolate, shredded or grated
5	teaspoons instant espresso powder		

In a medium metal bowl, whisk together the sugar, wine, and egg yolks. Make sure the eggs yolks are well blended. Place the bowl over a saucepan of boiling water and whisk constantly until the candy thermometer registers 170 degrees, about 4 minutes. Remove the bowl from atop the water, and whisk in the cheese in small pieces. Set aside to cool.

Lightly spray the sides and bottom of a 9-inch springform pan with nonstick cooking spray. In a medium bowl combine the 1½ cups hot water and the espresso powder, mixing well to dissolve the powder. Add the Kahlúa. Dip the ladyfingers into the espresso mixture and line the bottom and sides of the pan, completely covering the surfaces. Spread half of the custard mixture over the ladyfingers. Dip more ladyfingers into the espresso mixture and completely cover the custard. Pour the remaining custard over the ladyfingers. Refrigerate until firm, at least 4 hours or overnight.

When the ladyfingers are firm, beat the whipping cream at a medium-high speed until foamy, gradually add the confectioners' sugar, whipping until stiff peaks form. Too much whipping will turn the cream into a butter-like substance. Remove the sides from the springform pan. Fill a piping bag with whipped cream and pipe large rosettes around the outside edge of the tiramisu or with a large spoon drop whipped cream around the outside edge. Sprinkle shredded chocolate over the top of the tiramisu. Any leftovers should be stored in the refrigerator.

Makes 8 to 10 servings

Tip: To serve on a pretty plate, freeze the tiramisu overnight. Once frozen, remove the outside band of the springform pan and invert the tiramisu onto a clean flat baking pan and then invert again onto a pretty serving dish. Add the whipped cream and chocolate shavings before serving. Be sure to allow enough time to defrost.

MISS ANNE'S CHOCOLATE TRIFLE

Easy, delicious, and a crowd pleaser. The easiest way to make this cake is to purchase a box of chocolate cake mix, and bake the two layers according to directions.

1	(8-serving size) instant chocolate pudding mix	½	cup Amaretto liqueur, divided
3	cups cold milk	1	(16-ounce) container frozen whipped topping, thawed in the refrigerator
1½	layers chocolate cake, broken into bite-size pieces	3	Skor candy bars, crushed

Mix the chocolate pudding with the cold milk according to the package directions. Refrigerate to thicken. Layer half the chocolate cake pieces in the bottom of a trifle bowl (about a 2-quart capacity). Pour 1/4 cup of the Amaretto over the cake. Spread half the chocolate pudding mixture over the cake and amaretto. Spread half the whipped topping over the pudding. Sprinkle half the crushed Skor bars over the whipped topping. Repeat the layers, ending with the Skor bars. Refrigerate until ready to serve.

Makes 16 to 18 servings

Vanilla Ice Cream

Vicki and Bill Poston are members of the same Sunday school class I attend at First Baptist of Marietta. We always gather for a class Christmas party at the Postons' home, where we have lots of fellowship and food. This is one of their recipes.

4	large eggs, beaten	½	teaspoon table salt
3	cups sugar		Whole milk
½	pint whipping cream	2	cups crushed fruit, if desired
1	pint half-and-half		Bags of crushed ice
1	tablespoon vanilla	1	box rock salt

In a large mixing bowl beat the eggs until light and fluffy. Gradually mix in the sugar, beating at a medium-high speed until the mixture thickens. Add the whipping cream, half-and-half, vanilla, and table salt. Pour into a 4-quart ice cream freezer can. Add the whole milk to the "fill" line on the container. Churn according to the manufacturer's instructions.

Add 2 cups crushed fruit, if desired. (It is important to crush the fruit as they will freeze along with the ice cream and big chunks are hard to eat and not very flavorful when frozen hard.) Churn an additional minute or until the fruit is well combined.

Makes 1 gallon

TIP: If you are new to homemade ice cream, go to www.peasandcorn.com. The site has hints, recipes, and sell ice cream churns. I've made homemade ice cream many years and still found this site very helpful and remindful.

BUTTER PECAN HOMEMADE ICE CREAM

We've had three teachers for our Sunday School class over the last 40 years—Gene Ethridge, currently Dempsey Kirk, and Gary Bonds. Gary died several years ago, but we all remember his favorite activity for our class was the church's ice cream social. His special flavor was Butter Pecan. I cannot include ice cream recipes without remembering Gary, a faithful teacher and a man who loved and appreciated a good churn of homemade ice cream. His wife, Nancy, graciously shared his recipe.

2	cups pecans	3	(14½-ounce) cans evaporated milk
2½	cups sugar	1	tablespoon vanilla butternut flavoring
2	(3¾-ounce) packages instant vanilla pudding mix	2	quarts (8 cups) whole milk

Preheat the oven to 350 degrees. Spread the pecans on a baking sheet and roast 10 to 12 minutes, or until the pecans are slightly fragrant and just beginning to darken in color. Stir every 5 minutes. Cool, chop, and set aside. In a large mixing bowl, combine the sugar, the pudding mix, the evaporated milk, and the vanilla butternut flavoring. Pour the mixture into the can of a 6-quart ice cream freezer. Add the amount of whole milk needed to reach the "fill line" on the freezer container. Freeze according to the manufacturer's instructions, stopping about 10 minutes into the process to add the pecans. Continue the freezing process according to the manufacturer's instructions.

Makes 6 quarts (24 cups)

NOTE: For a 4-quart ice cream freezer, make half the recipe.

PEACH ICE CREAM

This delicious recipe comes from Executive Chef Tom McEachern.

6	medium peaches, peeled, pitted, cut into $\frac{1}{2}$-inch pieces (about 4 cups)
1	teaspoon lemon juice
	Pinch of salt
$2\frac{3}{4}$	cups sugar, divided
$2\frac{1}{2}$	cups whole milk

$2\frac{2}{3}$	cups heavy cream
2	teaspoons vanilla extract
$\frac{1}{4}$	cup vodka
4	mint leaves, sliced into ribbons
4	fresh, whole mint leaves

In a medium stainless-steel or glass bowl, combine the peaches, lemon juice, salt, and 1 cup of the sugar. Let stand for 1 hour. In a medium saucepan, scald the milk and the cream. Then add 1 cup of the sugar. In a small bowl whisk the remaining $3/4$ cup sugar and the egg yolks. Temper the milk with the egg yolks and continue to cook, stirring constantly over medium heat until thickened like a custard. Remove from the heat, strain immediately, and cool in an ice bath. Once the mixture is cooled, stir in the vanilla and transfer to refrigerator. In a large saucepan heat the softened peaches and the liquid, stirring over medium-high heat until the peaches are tender and the flesh is broken down. Transfer to a bowl, stir-in vodka, and refrigerate at least 4 hours or overnight. Strain the chilled peaches, reserving the liquid. Fold the ribbons of mint with the peaches. Stir the reserved peach liquid into the custard mixture. Pour into a 4-quart ice cream maker and follow the manufacturer's directions for ice cream churning, letting the container spin for about 20 minutes. Add the peaches, continuing to spin until combined (approximately) 1 minute. Transfer to a freezer container and freeze 2 hours before serving. Garnish each bowl with a fresh mint leaf before serving.

Makes 8 servings

TIP: To scald, heat milk to just below the boiling point.

TIP: To temper, slowly raise the temperature of the egg and sugar mixture by adding small amounts of the hot milk to it. Gradually adding about one-third to one-half of the hot liquid to the room temperature mixture prevents the egg from being cooked in the combining process. The tempered mixture can then be added back to hot liquid for the remaining cooking time.

ACKNOWLEDGMENTS

I can hardly believe that I am a published cookbook author. I have always loved reading cookbooks, planning meals, cooking new dishes, and entertaining. Many people have influenced me along the way. My mother, Frances Carol Heath Howell (I must give her complete name so I can see it memorialized in print), and my grandmothers, Charlye Ethel Paul Heath and Kate Zelpha McCluskey Howell, loved their families with all their hearts and labored with all their strengths. They not only passed on their knowledge of how to cook, but also the belief that strong family ties were nurtured around the dining room table. Their knowledge of and belief in a loving God has shaped my life.

It brings me a great deal of joy to acknowledge the loving and gracious acts of family, friends, and customers who played a role in bringing this book to fruition by believing in and encouraging me throughout the years. My daughters, Stephanie and Laura, you gave me every reason to provide a warm, loving home filled with good times good friends, and family. My husband Ed, you encouraged me with every recipe I tested, made numerous last-minute runs to the grocery for forgotten ingredients, and ferried food and dishes for photo shoots. Since this cookbook's inception, you have bragged unashamedly to anyone that would listen. There was no way that I could *not* make it happen after all your encouragement.

My "Birthday Club," a ladies monthly dinner group I've been eating with, laughing with, and—on occasion—crying with for the last thirty-one years, is responsible for some of the great recipes in this book. Thank you for swapping recipes with me for all these years. I cherish the memories! Estelle Bogle taught me to make homemade rolls and Sheilah King spent a morning with me cooking candy from recipes that might be a dying art.

Friends, too many to name here, tested and cooked dishes for me. Thank you all! Celebrity chefs, like Tom McEachern and Dennis Rowley, freely gave of their recipes, time, and expertise. Utmost Interiors, the beautiful shop next door to Gabriel's Desserts, loaned us Vietri dishes for our photo shoots. Thank you Rita Hall and Sharon Skipper for trusting us! You'll also see some of Paula Deen's dishes in the photos—that's just one of many things I thank her for. On the subject of photo shoots, we invaded the beautiful home of my friends Bill and Vicki Poston for three long days to get just the right light for some of the photography in this book. Good lighting was hard to find in the winter month of February, and the Postons were "lucky" enough to have just the light we needed.

I could not have taken the time to write this cookbook without help from the employees of Gabriel's Desserts. They baked and cooked and picked up the pieces for me when I was writing, editing, or doing a photo shoot—with never one complaint about all the extra work. What a team we have!

Since I am a newcomer to writing, many professionals have been at work on this endeavor: Emily Prather, who brought me to the good people at Thomas Nelson Publishers; Pamela Clements, who skillfully counseled me about the possibility of this coming together; and my editor-in-chief Geoff Stone who shared his extensive knowledge of the qualities of a good cookbook and figuratively held my hand for nine months. Using his creative mastery of editing and assembling—and reasonable but effective deadlines—he gave me the confidence to start and complete a project that I never thought I could do. Thank you, Geoff! Every person at Thomas Nelson Publishers has been an encourager and a true servant of this endeavor. Heather Skelton, Jason Jones, Jennifer Womble, and Scott Harris, I look forward to the road we have ahead!

Paula Deen, my loving and generous cousin, so many people love and respect you for the same reason I do: You share yourself and your love of life with everyone you encounter, making us believe that we, too, can be all that God intended us to be. You have counseled, encouraged, endorsed, and believed in me when I didn't even realize there was a reason to believe. God bless and keep you and yours always.

INDEX